A Town Called Charity

A Town Called Charity

And Other Stories About Decisions

Blaine M. Yorgason
Brenton G. Yorgason

Bookcraft

Salt Lake City, Utah

Library of Congress Catalog Card Number: 80-67358
ISBN 0-88494-408-5

First Paperback Printing, 1990

Lithographed in the United States of America
PUBLISHERS PRESS
Salt Lake City, Utah

For Dad,
a story-talker
who teaches,
with much love
and
respect

ACKNOWLEDGMENTS

We wish to thank our father, J. Gayle Yorgason, who helped us with the story *Old Zion*, and our dear friend, John Stoker, who, along with Ron Ellis, worked with us on the story *Acceptance*.

CONTENTS

PART ONE

FORCES FROM WITHIN

It has been said that the greatest battles ever fought are waged within the confines of one's own heart. We have been challenged to lift ourselves to the point where the Savior, Jesus Christ, can take us into the celestial kingdom. But we have also been given our agency and placed in a world where constantly we are forced to make decisions—decisions which move us either toward, or away from, our celestial goal. Frequently those decisions are painful, rarely are they easy. Yet all of us must make them.

The stories in this section discuss a few situations in which decisions must be made, and then examine some of the implications of those decisions. Perhaps you will recognize some of them.

THE SQUASH-BLOSSOM NECKLACE

The old stairs groaned loudly as David Michael Teague slowly descended them. Without even looking he knew that the ancient clock on the wall showed ten minutes past eight, and that meant he was ten minutes late opening up. Somehow, though, it just didn't seem to matter. In fact, it was getting hard to make anything really matter anymore.

At the foot of the stairs he paused to survey the long narrow room before him. Through the twilight of the still-drawn shades he let his eyes drift over the shelves, the half-empty shelves that held the sum total of his worldly goods.

A moment only he stood thus, for the prospects those shelves revealed were so discouraging that he could only think about them for a few moments without becoming terribly depressed, and David Michael Teague simply would not allow himself that fatal luxury. If he had little else, he at least had peace of mind in knowing that he was his own boss and was doing his best. It might not be that significant, but it was his best.

Quickly he ran a stanza of his favorite hymn, "The Day Dawn Is Breaking," through his mind. That hymn always made him smile, and as it did so once again he walked briskly to the front of the store to pull the shades and open the door to another and, he hoped, better day.

Sixty-seven dollars and eighteen cents! The grand total of yesterday's gross receipts. It was a good thing the rent on the old building was so low, and it was a good thing too that he could live in the room upstairs. He surely couldn't afford to live anywhere else.

He thought back to his mission for the Church a dozen years before. Funny, but it didn't seem that long ago. His mission had been wonderful, but at the time it had seemed to last forever. Now he had been home six times that long and he wondered where the years had gone.

Anyway, he could think of apartments he had lived in near the reservation that had seemed luxurious compared to his room upstairs. Still, the room was warm and the bed was soft, and what more could a man really ask for?

At the window he leaned over to grasp the pull on the shade, and as he did so he saw again the necklace placed carefully in the center of his window display. Halting then he stood for a moment gazing at it.

How that necklace stirred the depths of his soul! It was Apache silver and turquoise, delicately shaped in a squash-blossom pattern, and it was truly the most beautiful necklace he had ever seen.

He thought back to when, as a missionary, he had first met the old Apache who was, as he explained it, guardian of the necklace. Though knowing of the necklace, and being deeply moved by its beauty, Elder Teague had refrained from speaking of it to the old man for several weeks. While impatient by nature, he had learned the value of the Apache way, the way of deliberate slowness and thoughtful care. The necklace, he knew, had taken someone months to create. It was not something that he would wish to discuss immediately.

At last, however, the proper moment arrived. It was late, both he and his companion were seated cross-legged on blankets, and across the fire the old man sat silently, his necklace seeming to dance in the light of the fire.

Cautiously Elder Teague inquired about the necklace. After an appropriate moment of silence, the old man quietly spoke.

"*She-ke-sin,*" he said, "my young friend, at last it comes. You are truly becoming one with the people. I have seen your eyes glowing with eagerness like the stars are glowing in the star nations above. This Apache warrior congratulates you for the patience you have shown."

"Thank you, my friend," Elder Teague replied.

"But you have asked of the necklace, *She-ke-sin,* and I will tell you what I know. The necklace is old, much older than my grandfather. It has a life of its own, and a name. It is called *Yenta,* which, to the Apache, means matchmaker. Whether the necklace itself is Apache, this man does not know. It came to me as a youth. The wise one who hung it upon my shoulders prophesied that it would lead me to my *She-ah,* my wife, and that the necklace would bring peace to our lodge always. This it has done."

After months of close friendship with the old man, Elder Teague received his mission release. On the eve of his departure, knowing that he would likely never see his old friend again, he and his companion drove out to say good-bye.

Following a pleasant though emotional visit, Elder Teague stood to go. For a moment he and the old man clasped hands, and then with a sudden movement the old man removed the necklace and draped it around the neck of Elder Teague.

"My son," he said quietly, "this old man gives you *Yenta,* for thus the Spirit has directed. Treasure and protect it, and it will lead you to your *She-ah,* the one *Yenta* would have you find happiness with—one whose eyes are the color of these stones. Now go quickly, my son, in peace."

For over twelve years David had kept that necklace close to him, yet in all that time there had never been a girl with sky-blue eyes, nor a girl with any other color of eyes, for that matter. David Michael Teague was as alone today, if not more so, than he had been the day he was released from his missionary labors. *Yenta* had simply not worked.

Sixty-seven dollars and eighteen cents! What meager receipts for a shopping day just two days before Christmas. And that was why the necklace was in the window. David was broke, his rent long overdue. The necklace the old Apache had given him was the most valuable as well as the most beautiful item in his possession, and despite his own personal feelings about it, he desperately needed the money that its sale could bring. So now it was in the window, and when it was sold he would also sell a part of himself, the part that was wrapped around the sacred dream, which the old Indian had given him, of the girl with the sky-blue eyes.

As he reached down and pulled the shade, he was almost startled to see the small nose pressed against the fogged-up window pane. Almost, but not quite, for this was the third morning the little fellow had been standing there, waiting for the shades to be drawn so that he could see the necklace.

David unlocked the door and then walked behind the counter, anxiously considering how much he was counting on the sale of that necklace. It was almost humorous, too, especially when one considered that so far the only person who had shown any interest in the necklace was the little boy out front.

The day went fast, much faster than usual, for last-minute shoppers were scurrying around looking for the unusual or hard-to-find items that David seemed to have an affinity for when he went on his rare buying trips.

So it was a pretty good day as far as his days went, and he was satisfied, as he prepared to close the store, that his day's receipts would top a hundred dollars. Yes, and even more important, an elderly lady, with a dog which bore a remarkable resemblance to her, had been in the store and had expressed great interest in his squash-blossom necklace. She had promised that she would be in tomorrow to tell him definitely whether or not she would give him his desired price for it. What a Christmas present that would make for him! Why, with seven hundred dollars . . . .

The ringing of the bell above the door brought David's thoughts back to earth, and when he looked down he saw, standing across the counter looking up at him, the little boy who had stood at the window the three days previous.

"Hi," David said, smiling at the little guy whose eyes were not even level with the countertop. "May I help you?"

"Uh-huh. I wanna buy a necklace."

"A necklace, huh. Well, good! We have some very pretty necklaces here in this box, and you just tell me which one you want. This one is very pretty, and . . ."

"No, them ain't the ones. I want the one with the pretty blue rocks."

"Blue rocks?" asked David, already knowing what the child wanted.

"Uh-huh. The one over there in the window. It's for my sister; you know, for Christmas."

David smiled, deciding to humor the child. "For your little sis, huh?"

"Yeah," the boy beamed, "it's for sissie."

David's head whirled with a dozen questions, chief among them being who this little boy might be. He surely couldn't have that kind of money, but then one never knew. Maybe he could. But no . . . there was no way that. . . . Still, what harm could it do to show him the necklace up close, and then explain to him how valuable it was and that it was simply too expensive for him to buy.

Carefully David took the necklace from the window and placed it on the counter before the little boy, who stood motionless gazing at it for a long moment. Then, with a smile creeping across his face, he carefully stretched out one finger and gently caressed one of the smaller stones.

"Yep," he said happily, "that's the one, all right."

"It's pretty, isn't it," David said softly.

"Yep, real pretty."

"And expensive, too," David added, doing his best to make the word *expensive* sound significant to the child.

"Oh yeah," the boy sighed, "but I've got the money home on my dresser . . . all my nickels and dimes and quarters. I'll be back tomorrow to get it."

With that, the boy was gone, and David, smiling wistfully, picked up the necklace.

"*She-ke-sin,*" he thought suddenly. "I wonder what my old Apache friend would say if he knew I was trying to sell his necklace. If he knew my circumstances, I'm sure he would understand."

The next day, the last one before Christmas, was another slow one, and in the whole day he didn't turn over eighty dollars. Or he didn't until the lady with the matching dog came in and paid him the full seven hundred dollars he'd asked for the necklace. As David lifted it from the window and began wrapping it, he felt a strange tightening in his chest, and he saw before him, not the woman and the dog, but an old Apache Indian smiling at him across the flickering tongues of a small campfire.

"There you are, ma'am," he said emotionally. "I do hope you have a merry Christmas."

"Oh, I will," the woman beamed. "This will look so lovely. Thank you, son, and merry Christmas to you."

The last two hours of business dragged slowly, and it was just at closing time that the little boy came bursting through the door.

"I got the money, mister! You got my necklace wrapped?"

"I . . . a . . . well, son, I sold the necklace already."

"You . . . sold my necklace? But you couldn't! I told you yesterday I wanted it for sissie, and here's my money right here in my handkerchief."

As the little boy held up his handkerchief with the coins knotted inside, David saw that he was starting to cry.

"I'm sorry, son," David said simply, not knowing what else to do.

With a soft wail, the boy turned and ran from the shop. Already feeling terrible, David watched with mounting horror as the child darted into the path of an oncoming truck.

There was a screeching of tires, and in an instant David was kneeling beside the still and bleeding form of the child, who still clutched tightly the knotted handkerchief.

In a matter of minutes the ambulance carrying David and the boy arrived at the hospital. As the stretcher bearing the boy was rolled into the emergency room, David found himself being ushered to an office, where he began the frustrating process of admitting the boy.

"I don't know his name," David said for the third time. "He was just a customer in my store. Can't we ask him?"

"I'm sorry, sir, but as we have explained, he is unconscious . . . and a child must be signed in by a responsible adult. You'll have to sign for him, sir, and be financially responsible for his stay here."

Sensing the futility of argument, and hoping the boy's parents would pay the bill, he signed. As he did so, he smiled wryly, thinking that with his luck the boy would be an orphan and he would end up paying anyway. It would serve him right for selling the necklace in the first place.

It was two hours before the doctors came to the waiting room to discuss the boy's serious but stable condition. After the doctors had gone, David went to the boy's room and waited, hoping that the child soon would regain consciousness so that David could notify his family.

Early the next morning, as David was dozing in the chair, the door beside him quietly opened, and he found himself gazing into the bluest eyes he had ever seen.

"Bobby, is that you? Bobby, answer me . . . are you all right?"

Running to the bed, the young woman cradled the boy's head in her shaking arms. "Oh, Bobby," she said. "Please. Not you, too. You can't leave me here alone."

"Excuse me, ma'am," David said softly.

The woman turned, and through tear-filled eyes she questioned, "Who are you? And what are you doing here with Bobby?"

"I'm David Teague, ma'am. Bobby was in my store and I saw the whole thing. We didn't know your son's name, so there was no way we could contact you or your husband. He was in my store to buy a present for his little sister, but I had . . ."

At that moment Bobby coughed and opened his eyes, and the

woman, holding him close, broke into tears again, sobbing his name over and over.

Feeling decidedly uncomfortable, David was turning toward the door when the boy spoke.

"Sissie," he said, his voice sounding tiny and faraway, "I was going to get you a present, but the man already sold it, and I didn't get you nothing."

"Hush, Bobby. It's okay. I . . ."

"Sissie?" David asked startled. "Did he call you sissie?"

"Yes," she said, "of course he did. I'm his sister."

"But . . . but . . . I thought . . . well, I expected . . . but you're not little! And you're not his mother?"

"Well . . . I have been his mother since mom and dad died. But really, I'm just his sister."

David could not get over the woman's eyes. Her hair was auburn, framing a delicate yet bold oval face . . . but her eyes, her blue, blue eyes. Wistfully, David thought of the necklace, his squash-blossom necklace. The stones were the color of her eyes. "Oh," he groaned inwardly, "if only I hadn't sold . . ."

"But Sissie," Bobbie said, interrupting David's erstwhile thoughts. "What about Christmas? What am I going to get you for Christmas?"

"Bobbie, you don't have to get me anything. I've had a wonderful Christmas already. Just look at what my boss, Mrs. Hrebicek, gave me. She said that after five years I had earned this. Isn't it beautiful!"

And David Michael Teague stared in amazement as the woman quickly unwrapped her scarf and opened her coat, revealing *Yenta*, the matchmaker, David's squash-blossom necklace.

JACKS

The wind tore viciously at his coat as the twice-detained bishop slowly made his way through the blizzard to his waiting truck.

Thank goodness for a dependable vehicle, the bishop thought as he quickly cuffed away the snow from the frozen windshield.

Within seconds, eternally long seconds, Bishop Bailey found himself moving eagerly and yet apprehensively toward town on the icy road that he, himself, had helped build just three summers before.

"Come on, Bessy," he breathed, uncontrollably shaking from the freezing air being pumped through the still-chilled heater. "You can get me to that church if you're of a mind to . . . just keep on truckin'."

Ahead of him a car pulled onto the road, and the bishop recognized his young first counselor. *Wish I dared drive like he does,* the bishop thought. *No fool like a young fool. He's always in a hurry . . . it's a big thing for him to get there before I do, or so he says.*

The bishop continued to inch his way forward, watching his counselor's car disappear into the blizzard ahead.

Suddenly, and without warning, another car pulled out in front of the bishop. A new Lincoln Continental. The bishop hit his brakes and went into a slight skid while trying to avoid the other car, but by jockeying the wheel he maintained control of the old truck.

"Well, Brother Brown," he breathed, as his heartbeat slowed to normal, "you about got me that time. Course, maybe you didn't see me with all of that snow on your windshield. Looks like you're going to beat me to the meeting also. Fine thing, especially since I'm conducting, and you're the high councilor in charge."

For a quarter of a mile the cautious bishop drove carefully through the howling storm, but then the snow eased up a little. Suddenly the bishop saw ahead of him two sets of brake lights, and then a third set which was flashing. Creeping forward, Bishop Bailey quickly determined that a car was off on the shoulder of the road, and both his counselor and the high councilor were slowing as they approached it. As the bishop watched with interest and concern, his counselor spun around the stalled car and continued forward. *Close call, brother,* the bishop thought. *You're going too fast for your own good.*

The high councilor was next to approach the stranded vehicle. He paused for a moment, his car almost stopping, before he released his brakes and followed the ruts of the first car out around the stranded automobile. *Well, at least Brother Brown was able to slow down,* thought the relieved bishop. *Now I hope I can get around it as well.*

As he approached the stalled car, the bishop was surprised to see a huddled form trying to work a jack at the rear of the vehicle.

Hmm. I wonder why those brethren didn't stop, the bishop thought. *There's someone in trouble there.*

As he drew nearer still, he could tell that the form was that of a woman and that she was trying to change a flat tire.

For a moment he wondered again that the other two hadn't stopped, but then he realized that he couldn't stop either, for he was almost late for the opening meeting of his own ward conference.

Just then a gust of snow-filled wind battered against the bleak form of the woman, forcing her to drop the jack and huddle against the car for support.

"Good grief," the bishop mumbled, "I don't have time to stop, and I can't go on. What a day to have a flat tire!"

Bishop Bailey carefully nosed his truck in behind the woman's car, and then, taking a deep breath and pulling his collar up around his ears, he stepped out into the blizzard.

"Mornin', Sister," he shivered. "What seems to be the trouble?"

With a blank look on her face, the woman turned to stare at him, and the bishop, startled, realized that she was not one of his ward members.

"Fla . . fla . . flat tire," she stuttered, "and I . . I . . ca . . can't make my jack work."

Without reply, the bishop dropped to his knees and examined the jack, which he quickly determined was broken beyond repair. Still feeling embarrassed that he had called her "Sister" when he didn't even know her, the bishop forced a smile.

"You get in your car, ma'am, and keep warm. I'll get my jack out of the truck."

Working his way to his feet, the determined bishop made his way to his truck, only to find his new jack, his never-used jack, missing!

"Ryan," he groaned, thinking of his sixteen-year-old son's jalopy, "can't you ever put anything back where you got it?"

What do I do now? he wondered. *If I spend one more minute I'll be late, and oh, how I hate to be late! But I can't leave this lady here either. No matter who she is she's obviously got to have help, and there's no one here but me to do it.*

Working his way back to the woman's car, he tapped on her window and waited shivering while she lowered it. "Ma'am, my jack is missing. But there is a station down the road about a quarter of a mile. I'll go down there and borrow one and get it back to you. And don't worry, ma'am. You'll be on your way in no time."

Simply because the roads were so bad the drive to the service station took a little longer than Bishop Bailey thought it might. But worse than that, when he got there it was closed. And so, without even thinking, the bishop proceeded north to Tucker's station.

Relieved that he could see lights in the station, the bishop skidded to a halt, opened his door, and bolted across the ice-covered pavement and into the station.

The attendant on duty was a teenager, probably not much more than sixteen or seventeen.

"Hi," the bishop said, stamping the snow from his shoes. "There's a woman stalled back up the road a piece with a flat tire and no jack, and I was wondering if you had one, and if we could borrow it for a few minutes."

"No."

"What?"

"I said no."

"No, you don't have one, or no we can't use it?"

"No, you can't use it. We got one, but Tucker says no lending no tools to nobody."

"Son, I'm a bishop, and this woman needs help. You can trust me."

"Yeah, and I'm LaMar Grogen and you can trust me, too. But I'm sorry. I trust my boss the most. And he says if I lend out tools, I get fired. I believe him."

"But listen . . ."

"Mister, I said no. Can't do it. Now, if you can get the lady in here, I'd be happy to fix it for her, but that's the best I can do."

The phone rang, ending the conversation, and the bishop, thoroughly disgusted, slipped and slid back out to his truck.

Totally frustrated, he glanced at his watch. *Five minutes late. Oh no! . . . I've got to get to that meeting. Can't spend all morning chasing around the county for a fool jack! But doggone it, I can't leave that woman stranded either. Now let's see . . . where's the closest station?*

Turning onto the road, the bishop remembered the station on fifth street . . . *But that's self-serve,* he thought, *and they won't have a jack. Besides, it's probably closed this early on Sunday morning. And that leaves the station down by the freeway as my last chance. Mercy,* he thought, *that's a good four miles if it's one. Come on, Bessy, move it.*

It was twenty minutes before the frustrated bishop made it back to the woman's car with the borrowed jack and another ten before the tire was changed.

Gingerly, the bishop picked up the flat tire, trying to get it into the woman's trunk without dirtying his suit. But this Sunday morning was not his day. Just as he lifted the tire he slipped on a patch of ice, and down he went with the filthy tire on top of him.

"Oh, no," he said. "Why? Why me?"

Working his way from beneath the tire, he lifted it into the trunk and then stared in dismay at his grimy white shirt and increasingly gray suit.

"Sir," the woman called from her car window, "would you like me to return the jack? I'm going to the freeway. Is the station near there?"

The bishop, thinking of the fifteen-dollar deposit he had been forced to leave in order to get the jack, looked at his watch. *Just over forty minutes late,* he thought. *But hang the money. I've got to get to meeting!*

"Thank you, ma'am. I'd appreciate it greatly. The station is the one near the freeway."

"Thank you, sir. I don't know what I would have done if you hadn't stopped. My daughter went into the hospital this morning and I . . . well, thank you anyway."

The bishop, shivering, watched as she drove off. Then, grabbing a handful of snow, he hastily wiped off the worst of the mud from his now unsuitable suit.

It was seven minutes later when he walked through the doors of the chapel and with downcast eyes took his seat on the stand. The meeting was almost over and Brother Brown, the high councilor, was just making his way to the pulpit. As he passed the bishop he couldn't help but notice the grime and mud on the bishop's hands and clothes. *Disgraceful,* he thought. *How can a ward possibly respect a bishop who is so late for important meetings, and who comes looking so unkempt. Disgusting!*

Reaching the pulpit, Brother Brown smiled at Bishop Bailey and then addressed the congregation.

"Brethren, I would like to speak today on Luke 10:29-36. This is an area that we, your stake leaders, feel our members need help with. It is the well-known parable of . . ."

THE DAY THINGS GOT WORSE

If I hadn't been home that day, I'd probably never have known about what happened. For me, of course, it started the night before when I was coming home late from practice. I took a shortcut through the orchard with Shep, my dog, ran smack-dab into a skunk, and spent the rest of the night burying clothes, taking vinegar baths, and feeling sicker than I thought possible.

By the time the next morning rolled around I looked and felt like death warmed twice, and so I had no trouble talking mom into letting me stay home from school. Add to that the fact that, according to dad, I still smelled like I had a stripe on me, and you'll understand why I had no desire to go to first-period math class and sit next to Sheri, who had to be the most beautiful girl in the school. It was difficult enough trying to impress her even when I smelled good, and so that day I simply stayed home sick and got to know my mom.

It was still full dark when I heard mom's alarm clock sound off, and that seemed to start the whole thing. Now you should know that her clock isn't one of those sweet-sounding things you see on commercials. Nor does it have a snooze button. What it does have is a raucous-sounding screecher that mom says was invented by the devil to awaken the damned in a very warm place. I don't know about that, but it surely does pull her out of bed. It did me too, that day. And everyone else as well.

Once I asked mom why she had to get up so early, and she mumbled something about her hair. She says some women can sleep three weeks solid standing on their heads, wreck a half-dozen cars, get abducted at gunpoint by bankrobbers, go over Niagara Falls in a barrel, and walk away from the whole thing looking like they just left their hairdressers. Not my mom! Thirty minutes on a pillow and she looks like she had stuck her finger in a light socket. A whole night and it's hard to tell her apart from a major disaster at sea. She says she loves dad and wouldn't want him to go into cardiac arrest every morning. Neither would she want us kids calling the animal control shelter each day. Besides, she likes to spend some time on her knees getting braced for the day, or so she says. And so, off goes her alarm at 5:00 A.M. sharp . . . that day like every other before it.

Normally the rest of us, all except for the triplets, stagger out of bed at about six o'clock for scripture study. Some days we have it, while some days things get started wrong with mom and dad refereeing the third world war or something, and some days we just don't get in gear in time for it. That day was no different . . . a combination of chaos and mental cobwebs prevailed.

I awakened to the screeching of mom's alarm and immediately groaned in agony, knowing I was too sick for travel, even if it was a matter of blocks to my school. Feeling dizzy and once again sick to my stomach, I made my way into the bathroom. As if being sick wasn't enough, Patty, my sister, became furious because I was in the bathroom and she needed to put on her face. Two of the triplets, who aren't quite two, woke up crying, which awakened the third, and all three of them started up like a chorus of fire engines. That woke up Johnny, who is four, and Mindy, who is six, and you'd have thought we were going to the Fourth of July

parade the way the family was running around yelling and hollering.

Well, mom didn't have time for her knees or her hair, for all
three triplets had to have their diapers changed and Johnny should
have had one on. Dad and Patty had to leave early and so there
wasn't time for mom to fix them much of a breakfast, or for them
to help her either, for that matter. Mom did ask Patty to help fix
the sandwiches for dad's lunch, but Patty groaned about being late
for cheerleading practice, and that was that.

I kind of lost track of things then as it was all I could do to
stagger from the couch to the bathroom and back again, just in
time to repeat the trek, and so I wasn't much help either. Add to
that the fact that Mindy was on a spunk about something, and all
she would do was sit in the middle of the kitchen floor and yell.

All in all it was an exciting morning, and it wasn't too difficult
to sense that mom was gradually losing control of her own
emotions as well as the entire household. Every time she said something, which was about every thirty seconds, her voice would raise
an octave. I've never heard mom swear, but it looked to me like
she was getting set to let out with a string of words that would
sizzle bacon.

By the time dad was ready to leave, the triplets had gone
through three more diapers and had clogged the toilet trying to
flush one of the diapers down. In addition, they had pulled all the
clothes out of their dresser and then had systematically pulled all
of the books out of the bookshelf in dad's study. While mom was
putting their clothes away, they spilled a ten-pound sack of flour
onto the kitchen floor; and while mom was salvaging as much flour
as she could, they quietly emptied the clothing from Johnny's
dresser. I'll tell you, mom was one lady not to fuss with right then,
and so there I sat in total silence.

As he was leaving, dad gave mom a squeeze, and by way of
consolation, I suppose, told her not to worry, that things could be
worse. It was then that mom gave way with a bucket of tears, and
although dad tried his best to console her, it wouldn't stop those
tears. Mom said she didn't want consolation; she wanted help and

sympathy. And if not that, she wanted an M-1 rifle, fully loaded. I could tell by then that it was not a good day for me to stay home from school!

Well, when mom wouldn't be consoled, dad threw up his arms in frustration and headed for the car. Patty was waiting for him, and she looked as if she was ready to boil, she was so mad. Oh, she was late alright, but at least she could be thankful she was getting out of the house!

What a morning that was! Too sick to work my way back up to my bedroom, I had to just lay on the couch and watch the hours bang and scream by. One of the triplets pulled a burning log out of the wood stove, Johnny located dad's shaving stuff, got cream all over the bathroom and cut his face up something awful, one of the triplets emptied the pencil sharpener all over the kitchen floor, Mindy still wouldn't stop crying, and the phone rang every three minutes.

Mom had promised the Relief Society president that she would make a batch of bread for their social, both clothes hampers were jammed full and needed her attention, and the visiting teachers were coming any minute. Like dad said, things could get worse, and they did just that.

In the middle of her bread, mom remembered that she was out of yeast, and so she left me in charge while she went down the lane to the neighbors. For the first three minutes I was fine, but then I had to attend to some personal needs in the bathroom. By the time I returned to the couch mom was home, and boy oh boy! In the eleven minutes she was gone, and the eight or so that I was in the bathroom, the triplets and John had squeezed out a whole tube of toothpaste onto the kitchen counter. They had spilled all of Mindy's medicine, which they had been trying to give her so she would stop crying, they had unrolled a roll of adhesive tape around the kitchen chairs, and they had dumped the better part of a can of Ajax on the floor while trying to clean up the mess from the pencil sharpener. Mom became somewhat excited, but me . . . well, I was kind of impressed. Golly, at least they were trying to be helpful. I didn't point that out though. Believe me, I didn't! By the time a guy is my age, he'd better know when to keep his mouth shut. I do, and I was silent as a tree full of owls at noontime.

Anyway, mom finally got her bread into the oven just when the doorbell rang announcing the visiting teachers. She turned to answer it and found one of the triplets toddling toward her across the kitchen floor, dragging a soggy diaper from one foot, leaving a trail behind it. Mom was taking a quick swipe at cleaning that up when there was a sudden lot of screaming and barking at the front door. Seconds later we discovered that Shep had dug up my skunked clothing and was trying to present it to the visiting teachers. They were not on a Deseret Industries drive that day, however, and so they were well down the lane, still screaming and still running, with Shep right behind them, when I got to the porch and was able to call Shep back.

Well, I was rousted out for burial detail again, and after a little while I had both Shep and my clothes out of sight, and I guess out of smell.

I was surprised that the visiting teachers came back to the house, but they did, and as I entered the front door I stopped to catch my breath, and in doing so heard their lesson. If you can believe it, the lesson turned out to be about how LDS women ought to be running their homes. They read off some list about the way true Latter-day Saint mothers should keep their homes clean, have an attractive and peaceful atmosphere, prepare nutritional meals, have beautiful table settings, start stimulating conversations during meals, sew and quilt for their own and for their neighbors' needs, study the scriptures thirty minutes a day, spend thirty minutes a day on their knees, keep a daily journal, attend the temple twice a month, do genealogical research, write letters regularly to missionaries, shut-ins, and relatives, get adequate rest, do thirty minutes of exercises in addition to fifteen minutes of waist and tummy flatteners, be beautiful, teach their children the gospel, teach them to be honest, obedient, industrious, talented, clean, healthy, safe, sensitive to nature, creative, and teach them to clean their teeth, and to prepare good talks. In addition they should support their PTA, political party, symphony guild, writer's guild, and current mother's march. They should develop their own talents in music, art, dance, and tennis. They should read good literature, should take time to listen to all of the interesting "guess whats" of their children, should make certain that each of the children learn to play an instrument, and have them active in the seasonal sports programs. In addition, they should greet their husband at the door each evening looking as fresh and exciting as a morning daisy.

When they finished reading, the two sisters laughed, but not mom. She either burst a gasket or had a seizure, for at that point she staggered out of the room all red and purple.

The sisters, genuinely concerned, asked me what was wrong. I didn't dare tell them the whole truth, so I just said that we were all coming down with incipient hoof-and-mouth disease, which was terribly contagious, and mom was showing the first symptoms. Well, those two ladies left in somewhat of a hurry, as I would have done in similar circumstances, and then I heard mom crying.

I looked back into the kitchen, and the triplets apparently had decided that the wash and the bread were both done. There in the middle of the kitchen floor were mom's sopping wet wash and each of the seven loaves of almost-baked bread, upside down and pulled out of the pans. And in the middle of the floor knelt mom, crying like she was a little lost girl.

I didn't know what to do, so I went in and hugged her and then went into the bedroom where I hit my knees for a little guidance. I don't know exactly what I wanted Heavenly Father to do, maybe send down a legion of angels or something, but none came, and after my prayer the only thing I could think to do was to call dad.

Quietly I told him all about mom's day and about how things had gotten worse. For a long time he was silent, and then he thanked me for calling and hung up. About thirty minutes later, just as mom and I were starting in on the kitchen floor, the doorbell rang. Mom rolled her eyes in dismay, opened the door, and there stood dad, wearing a new apron and carrying about a hundred long-stemmed roses. Without a word he walked in, kissed her softly, put the roses into her arms, and went to work. And he'd just barely gotten started when the doorbell rang again. Once more mom opened it, and there stood Patty, smiling sheepishly.

"Hi, mom," was all she said, then she walked in, put on another apron, and joined dad in the kitchen. Well, not wanting to be out-done I put on another apron, and mom just stood there staring at all of us, standing quieter than a hole in the ground. Then she started laughing, or crying, or both, I don't know which, and we all joined in.

It was a great way to end the day things got worse.

PAYING DUES

When was the last time you went fishing with dad?"

The question, totally unexpected, caused my mind to make a complete revolution. In the gathering dusk I peered more closely at my younger brother, trying to determine why he had asked it. But so far as I could tell, his expression hadn't changed at all. His husky frame still relaxed comfortably in the webbed lounge chair, his finger continued to trace circles around the top of his long-empty diet soda can, and he still gazed at the looming mountain known locally as Squaw Peak.

Fishing, I wondered? How long since I had been fishing with dad? And why had Greg thought of that? We had been talking about our family business and some of the problems we were encountering as we worked to develop trust between family members who had drifted apart by almost as many years as they had miles. Greg and I, though separated greatly by age, were still very close, and the more I came to know him the more impressed I

became with his wisdom, his sense of justice, and his deep understanding of things spiritual. And thus I questioned the motive for
his question, trying to comprehend what he meant, not understanding how going fishing with dad was related to family trust.

"I don't know, Greg. Five, six years, maybe. Why?"

"How well do you remember it?"

"What do you mean?" I laughed.

"Details, brother. Do you remember any details about your last
fishing trip with dad?"

"Well, some, I guess. I remember it was a Saturday, and dad
and I and my two oldest boys pulled dad's boat up to Strawberry,
where we spent most of the day fishing."

"Did BYU have a game that day?"

"Uh . . . yes, I think they did."

"Who caught the first fish?"

"Why, I think it was . . . no, wait a minute. It was dad. I remember, because he made a bet with Nate, Nate lost, and he
wasn't too happy about it. Dad went to the game while Nate had
to mow his lawn, or something like that."

"Aha! You see, that's what I'm talking about."

"What? Greg, you aren't making any sense."

"Sure I am. Let me tell you about my last fishing trip, or most
any of them for that matter. You know how dad loves to fish, and
you probably also know that he isn't exactly an expert fisherman.
Am I right?"

I nodded, grinning, and Greg continued.

"Whenever dad and I went fishing, we'd get out on the water
and I'd hurry and get my lure in first so I could beat dad with the
first fish. And then I'd offer to bet him that I would catch it, too.
But he never would bet, not on anything right then. That frustrated
me, because sometimes I caught the first fish, and I caught it in a
hurry. When that happened, dad just smiled and told me what a
great fisherman I was, and that was the end of it.

"On the other hand, if both of us went for a long time with no
fish, then dad would casually ask if I was ready to bet. I'd ask what

he had in mind, and it was usually something pretty valuable, like the opportunity to use their season tickets and escort mom to the BYU ballgame that afternoon.

"Well, you know me. I'm the eternal optimist. I'd agree, we'd shake on it, and then dad would go into his ritual. He'd drop his head, hold his forehead in his hand for a moment or two, start up the engine, move to another spot on the lake, change lures, and pull in the first fish. Almost every time! Do you remember him doing that?"

"Yes, a few times, after I was older. But Nate and Steve tell me he does it all the time with them. I think it's funny."

"Funny? Well, I didn't. For years I didn't think it was fair. Why should he be able to pray and . . . ?"

"Pray? What do you mean?"

"You know what I mean. I used to wonder why dad could simply drop his head and pray and have the Lord tell him where to go and what lure to use to catch the first fish. Would you think that was fair?"

"Well, no. I . . ."

"I even prayed myself, but God never told me where to go or what lure to use. For years that bothered me, but then one day, when I was sitting home cleaning fish while dad and mom were enjoying a ballgame, the answer came to me. And when it did, I vowed then and there to one day be able to do what dad did."

Greg was silent for a few moments, evidently assuming that I knew what he had vowed to do. But I didn't, and so at length I asked, still wondering what all this had to do with our family.

"You really don't know," Greg responded? "Why, I vowed to pay my dues, just like dad had."

"What?"

"Oh come on, don't be so thick. Dad's righteous, and you know it. He always does what he's supposed to do, says what a good man ought to say, and I imagine he thinks mostly righteous thoughts.

"You see," Greg continued, "by being righteous as much as he could, dad paid his dues to the Lord. He was willing to trust God totally, in terms of obedience, and that was why I guess Heavenly Father was willing, after a time, to tell dad where and how to catch that first fish. It is the same with everything we do, brother. If you want something badly enough, you go after it. You pay your dues. Like our family, which we want to be close. It won't be until we've all paid our dues, until we've practiced trust without questioning, and so on. No backbiting, no being petty, and no reminding of small debts owed and small favors unreturned.

"That day when I vowed to pay my dues to the Lord was a turning point in my life. Since then I've done my best, or usually I have, to be obedient to the commandments as I have understood them. And now I am starting to receive dividends. I still don't get impressions telling me where to catch the first fish, but the other day I felt impressed to wait at a stop sign longer than usual, and because I did I was not involved in a deadly accident that occurred in that very intersection not ten seconds later.

"There have been other occurrences, too. Just little things, but they aren't as important as the principle behind them. You see, dad taught me to pay my dues, I have tried, and so the Lord is allowing me to join his spiritual organization, so to speak. In that same way, our family will only be close when we've joined up and paid our dues.

"Well, what do you think?"

To tell the truth, I was nearly speechless. Greg was right, of course. Once again I was impressed with his wisdom, his insight, and his depth of understanding. Then too, at last I felt I understood how it had all come about. Like he had modestly declared, Greg had paid his dues.

It was full dark now, and in the softness of the night I grinned, recalling my own memory of dad's bowed head, and wondering if I ought to tell Greg about it. On that last fishing trip I'd asked dad what he was doing when his head was bowed, and with a sly grin he'd told me of a book he had once read, something about how to catch the big ones in Strawberry. All he was doing, when he bowed his head, was recalling where the book said to go and what it said to use for a lure. Dad was exercising his memory, not his faith.

Yet now my grin grew even wider, and I knew I wouldn't tell Greg, then or ever. For there was nothing to tell him, nothing at all. In fact, he was right, and it was as simple as that. Dad *had* paid his dues.

DIALOGUE OF LOVE

Mike braked his car to a stop in the parking lot, turned off the ignition, and took a deep breath.

"Well, elder," he said, grinning at his son through the rearview mirror. "This is it. The MTC. Nineteen years your mom and I have watched you prepare for this day. Therefore let us not tarry, but make haste to remove thy bags from the trunk that thy departure may be swift and thy journey secure."

Mike glanced at his wife Karma to see if his attempt at humor had helped her tears. She caught his glance, sniffed and smiled, and shot right back at him.

"And it came to pass," she said laughingly, "that they went and did as they were commanded."

Together the three of them laughed, climbed out of the car, and began unloading the luggage. As they did so a car pulled in beside them, the door opened, and another young elder, almost awkward in his new suit, climbed out.

"Hi," he said shyly.

Mike and his wife smiled and said hello, and their son Travis stepped over, shook hands, and introduced himself. For a moment they talked together, and then the two of them approached Travis's parents.

"Mom and Dad, this is Elder Jason Wheelright. Elder Wheelright, my parents, Mike and Karma Jenkins. Elder Wheelright and I are going to the same mission."

Elder Wheelright smiled shyly and shook hands with Mike and his wife.

"I'm pleased to meet you," he said. Then he turned to look at the woman getting out of the passenger side of his car.

"Mom, come and meet these folks. Their son and I are going to the same mission."

The woman, pulling a package from the back seat of the car, turned and came toward them, smiling.

"Sister Jenkins," Elder Wheelright said, "this is my mother, Cindy Wheelright. Brother Jenkins . . . this is my mother."

Mike, leaning into the trunk to pull out some luggage, turned smiling and then stared, almost dropping the suitcase he was holding.

"Hello . . . Cindy," he managed, holding out his hand to shake hers. *Cindy,* he thought. *Cindy Stewart!*

"Mike? Mike Jenkins? My heavens, is it really you? Why, I haven't seen you since, well . . . since the summer you got home from the army."

"Karma," Mike said, turning to his wife, "Cindy and I went to high school together. We even dated. In fact, as I remember," he said, grinning and for some reason feeling embarrassed, "we went steady for nearly a year." And then he thought:

And what a year that one was!

Cindy laughed, flushed just a little, and nodded in agreement. Her smile, Mike noted, was exactly like that of her son.

"That's right," she said. "Mike Jenkins, star of our championship debate team, was my first true love. And to think that now our sons are going to the same mission field. What a small world we live in!"

For the next hour both families were busy with registration and orientation. Following that, and some very tearful good-byes, Mike and Karma started toward the foyer. The tears of happiness and loneliness had not helped Karma's face, however, and so she excused herself and went to the ladies' room.

Mike, waiting in the foyer, suddenly realized that Cindy was standing next to him, drying her own tear-stained cheeks.

"It's hard, isn't it," she said, "sending a son away for so long. I didn't know if I could go through with it."

> *But Mike isn't crying. I wonder if he feels it like I do?*

"It sure is, Cindy. For a few minutes there I was worried about Karma. She had a hard time."

> *I did, too, I guess. But it just doesn't show as much with me. Right now I'm glad, though. I think I'd be embarrassed, with Cindy standing here.*

"She's pretty, your wife. Where did you meet her?"

> *She really is, too. I never was that pretty. No wonder he married her.*

"We met at school. I don't remember if you ever told me where you met your husband."

> *I can't believe how very little Cindy has changed! She's a bit heavier, but her face hasn't changed at all.*

"My husband was a blind date, Mike. It was really funny how we met. From the start we both knew it was right. Is Travis your oldest son?"

> *My goodness but Mike has gained weight. I'll bet he's gained fifty or sixty pounds. I didn't recognize him until I heard his voice. And to think he used to brag about how he was always going to be skinny.*

"Yes, Travis is the oldest of five sons. But we did get two daughters, too. How about Jason? Is he your oldest?"

> *Her smile is still as pretty as it always was. I'll never forget how she could make me happy on my bluest days just by smiling at me.*

"Our oldest son, but not our oldest child. We do have an older married daughter, and after Jason was born we had another daughter before my husband was killed. I never remarried."

> *Mike must have stayed active in the Church. I often wondered if he would. Some days he surely had a bad attitude.*

"I'm sorry, Cindy. I didn't know about your husband."

> *I . . . Good grief! I sure did put my foot into the old mouth that time. I wonder why she never remarried. She's certainly attractive enough to arouse plenty of interest.*

"Mike, it's all right. I know you didn't know. That's why I told you. Besides, it's been a long time now. It doesn't hurt much anymore. You helped me get past that, you know. You told me once that good-bye, like death, was inevitable. But love, like resurrection, was more ultimate. I loved my husband. Ultimately we will be together. That's also why I never remarried. I've felt no need to.

"Say, do you remember that night when we won the state basketball tournament, and you piled fourteen of us into your car? We all got in but Lynn Barnes, who rode all the way home on the back bumper."

> *And I was snuggled up so close to Mike that I could hardly breathe. I thought I'd die, I was so excited. That was the night I fell in love with him.*

"Yeah, I remember, alright. How could I forget that night? Lynn Barnes, Steve Ockey, and Jim Garrett. I haven't thought of them in years. I wonder how they are doing?"

> *Boy, do I remember that night! Cindy was practically on my lap the whole trip home, and did I ever want to kiss her. Almost did, too, but I just didn't dare. I wonder if she wanted to kiss me?*

"I don't know, Mike. I haven't seen them at all. And do you remember our junior prom? That was the most exciting dance I ever went to. Mother made me a whole new outfit for that dance, and you and I danced the whole night together."

> *Dad bought me those new high heels, too, and . . . oh, my aching feet! I twisted my ankles and you bruised my toes all night long.*

"Sure, I remember the prom. That was a special night."

> *And an expensive one, too. I spent all the money I had on tickets and flowers, and had to borrow Kent Peterson's new suit because I didn't have one and couldn't afford one either. Kent even loaned me his new tie and tie tack. But then, being with her made it worth every penny.*

"We certainly had a lot of fun that year."

> *And when it ended, and he left for the army, I thought I'd die.*

"Hey, Cindy, I was in Los Angeles last year and you'll never guess who I ran into. It was Mary Ellen and her husband."

> *Man, I wonder where Karma is? She should be back by now. I can't believe how nervous this makes me, talking with Cindy. You'd think I was a young kid trying to get my first date.*

"Mary Ellen? Did you really? I hear from her once in awhile, but I haven't seen her in ages. Do you remember the time when you almost set your dad's haystack on fire?"

> *I wonder where his wife is? I hope my hair is still in place. My knees are shaking and I can't understand why. Maybe I'd better go.*

"Do I ever remember that fire! But I also remember that you almost burned down your aunt's home when you took out the hot ashes and left them next to the door, causing it to catch on fire."

They both laughed, and then Mike thought:

> *What am I nervous for? I don't need to be nervous. This is Cindy, my high school sweetheart. I loved her once. Why should things be so different now?*

"Cindy, I've thought about you over the years, wondering where you were and how you were doing. Are you happy, Lady?"

> *I hope she is. She certainly deserves happiness for the rich start in life that she gave me.*

"Lady? Do you know I haven't been called that in years? Yes, I'm very happy. I couldn't have a better family, and that is what is important. It's funny, but the other day I thought of that letter you sent me when you were in the army. I memorized that letter, and I can still quote it after all these years. You said the funniest things, but the part I remember best, the part that makes me feel good, even now, was when you said:

> Avocado sandwiches are where it's at. You are the light of men, the supreme angel in every choir I've ever heard or seen. You know, if I were home I'd come skipping to your door with a long-stemmed rose and whap you with it. *Whap! Whap!* And then I'd stoop to brush the dented petals from your step and then rise slowly to meet your eyes with a steady gaze and say, Lady, I love you!

"Mike, you've no idea how many times that special silly letter has taken me through another day."

> *Oh, I hope so much that he understands what I am trying to say. He was always so gifted with words, and I never could say what I thought.*

"It's funny, Cindy. I don't remember that letter, but I do remember my feelings. Thoughts of you helped me through my military experience. Even after you wrote of your engagement, when I was on my mission, I kept you in mind. Perhaps not *you* really, but the fine ideal of you that always uplifted me."

> *My goodness, but I am having some interesting feelings. After all these years I find that I still have special feelings for Cindy. Not like those I have for Karma, of course, for she is my celestial companion. But one night Cindy taught me the real meaning of love, giving me purpose and direction at a time when I had neither. I remember that night vividly. I could have been tempted, but I thought so much of Cindy that I knew I could not allow either of us to do anything that would bring pain or shame to her. That night I learned that the difference between desire and love was simply the difference between selfishness and caring. Cindy helped me see that holding the priesthood was a commitment to love and to care. Because of her strong values, I will always appreciate her greatly. I wish there was a way to tell her, to thank her.*

"My engagement? Do you remember that? Did you know that

you wrote me another letter then, and I memorized part of it, too. Would you like to hear it?"

"Sure, I guess."

> *How in the world could she remember all this? I can't even remember writing it!*

"You wrote:

Your engagement says something fine about the man, but it's doing things to my mind. I hope that your excitement is an overestimation and that you will promptly relegate the fellow to complete social freedom. However, you shouldn't be flippant, Lady. Either be with him or be without him, but don't play with his emotions. A man's dignity is a fine and fragile thing, far more precarious in courtship than in slavery. And for a girl to be a woman, she must respect that dignity beyond social gambits or coquettish games. However, if you can chuck him into the lake without damaging his dignity — go straitway and say, 'Be thou removed, be thou cast into the sea.' Lady, at this tiny point of time in eternity you are my favorite woman. Never forget that!

"Mike, I don't know why this is so hard for me to say, but I'm so proud to have been your friend, to have been a small part of your life. I . . . well, I leaned on your moral strength, and that ultimately led me to my husband."

> *And it really did, too. There was that one night especially when we could have made a terrible mistake. I wonder if Mike remembers that? I remember that he pushed himself away from me, and then we talked of purity and priesthood and of promises we had made regarding virtue. Mike made me feel so clean and pure that I have never since dared let him down. That night I learned the meaning of priesthood covenants, and that understanding, taught me so awkwardly and yet so beautifully by Mike, helped me to recognize the same power of goodness in my husband when I met him. For that one night of righteousness alone, I will respect Mike forever.*

"Thank you, Cindy. You've said exactly what I have felt. I hope you know, Lady, that I love you still."

And I'm sure I always will.

"Thank you, Mike. I will always have a special love for you, as well."

At that moment Karma Jenkins appeared in the hallway, and Cindy, seeing her approach, walked to her and took hold of her hands.

"Sister Jenkins . . . Karma, you must be a very special woman, and I'm so thankful to meet you. I hope you understand when I tell you that I loved your husband once because of the boy that he was. I love him even more now because he is the man you have helped him become. I do hope we can stay close through our sons. God bless you both."

The two women silently embraced, and then Cindy, after taking Mike's hand for a brief moment, turned and walked out of the door.

THE DECISION

The old woman stirred restlessly in her bed and then cringed as the pain grabbed her stomach and twisted it into knots. Desperately she fought back the tears in her eyes and the cry in her throat, and after a dozen eternities it began to subside. Carefully then, and slowly, she stretched her legs until they were straight. Gently, she took hold of the protecting bars on the sides of her bed and pushed her body around until it too was straight, aligned once again with the configuration of the bed.

Another one! That was the third attack in less than an hour. The doctor had been right, then. He'd said that the attacks would grow in numbers and intensity, and that just before the end they would slack off, letting her die in peace. The old woman appreciated the doctor leveling with her like he had done. She'd known she was dying, but it was comforting in a way to hear it from someone else. That somehow made it a little easier to face. Besides, she'd been facing things alone for so long now that it was nice to finally be able to share.

The afternoon sunlight fell through her window and trailed across her bed, and with a gentle flick the old woman set free from her blanket a few dozen dust particles that tumbled helter-skelter up into the shaft of light. With a smile that she knew would never pass for one, she watched the dance of the dust, a dance that she had first seen under the careful hand of her mother so many long years before. How many times now, she wondered, would she be able to watch that special little dance and find joy in the absolute freedom of the tiny specks of dust? Perhaps soon she would be like them, free and unfettered.

Another terror grabbed her middle and she felt herself drawing into a tight little ball to combat the pain, and it was when it finally subsided that she became aware of the screaming siren approaching the hospital. She had never liked sirens, though goodness knows she had had ample opportunity to get used to them those past few weeks. Yet she hadn't, for she knew that each represented a person, a human being just like herself, who was even at that moment crying out against unbearable pain, inflicted upon them almost randomly and with no thought at all for their own wishes.

Just like her own pain. She would never have wished for it, and certainly could not say that she enjoyed it. Still, it was hers, and from experience she knew she could live with it, could cope with its own particular methods of torture. In fact, when she thought of the pain others must be feeling, she was thankful that she had her own and could not trade it off. A woman never knew what she might get herself into by trading.

Hours later, her troubled sleep was disturbed by a soft light and the sound of muffled voices, and she knew that they were bringing someone in to use the other bed in her room. She wanted to protest, as she had definitely requested a private room, but she was too groggy to do anything except moan a bit and then fall back into the blackness of sleep. Besides, in the morning . . .

But the woman in the other bed was not a woman at all, just a little girl. Why in thunder had they brought a girl in here? In the morning light the old woman studied her carefully. She was lying on her back, a giant cast covering her from her neck down past her hips. Her legs and one arm were held aloft by ropes and braces, and she looked like some giant disabled crab hanging there.

Her eyes were closed, so the old woman assumed she was asleep, though how she could ever sleep like that she couldn't even guess. Turning then she gazed out the window, wondering how long they would leave the girl there before moving her. It wasn't that she didn't want company, it wasn't that at all. It was just that, well . . . she simply didn't want anyone to see her lose control when the pain finally became too intense during her last few days. She had already lost enough of her dignity, and she didn't have much left. What little of it there was she wanted preserved intact. It was that simple, and it did not seem to her a very great request.

Yet move the girl they did not. The hospital was too full, and for two days the old woman endured in silence her helpless intruder. On the morning of the third day, though, as she was coming out of perhaps her worst attack, the little girl finally broke the silence.

"Does it hurt pretty bad?"

"Excuse me?"

"Uh . . . I just wondered if you were hurting very badly."

"Why? Did I act like it hurt or something?"

"Well, no. But gee, I can tell it hurts a lot, and I was thinking maybe I could call a nurse for you . . . or something."

"No, I don't want a nurse. A nurse couldn't do much anyway. Like they say, this thing is bigger than all of us."

"What do you mean?"

"The big one, girl. I've got the big one. There isn't a thing anyone can do for me now. I've got cancer clear from my chin right down to my toenails, and right this very minute I'm in the middle of my final countdown."

When there was no further response from the girl, the woman turned to look at her and was surprised to see tears streaming down her face and soaking into the pad that supported her chin.

"Say, why are you crying? Are you in pain too?"

With an effort the girl brought up the one arm that she had use of in an effort to wipe away the tears, and the old woman realized with a start that she had embarrassed the girl. Only trouble was, she didn't know how to retract her question.

For only a moment the girl struggled, and then with a choking voice she replied.

"No, ma'am, I'm not in pain. At least not too much. I guess I'm feeling guilty and ashamed is all. I didn't mean to start bawling and . . ."

"Now, hold on there. You don't need to feel ashamed."

"Yes I do. You see, ma'am, for the past two days I have been laying here feeling sorry for myself because my back is broken and I won't be able to get out and around for a few months. I've also been thinking," and now the words tumbled out rapidly, "that it was a shame they used valuable hospital space for old hypochon-driacs like you."

"Hypochondriacs?"

"Yeah, can you believe that? For some reason that was all I thought was wrong with you, and now I find that after all my bad thoughts here you are dying, and . . ."

"Hey, don't take it so hard. How were you to know? Besides," and now the old woman chuckled, "I've been wondering the same things, about what an old woman like me is doing in a place like this. Why, if I was the doctor I'd get rid of me, and fast too, believe me."

They both laughed then, and the tension eased.

"Ma'am," the girl asked a moment later, "if you're dying, how come your family doesn't come to see you?"

"Family? I've got no family. There's no one but me."

"Oh, come on. Everybody has a family."

"Not me! Not this old hypochondriac."

The girl was surprised at the bitterness in the woman's voice, and she twisted her neck in the cast to look more closely at her.

"Don't get me wrong, young lady," she continued. "I had a family once. In fact, I had three of them. Or at least three hus-bands. I may not look it now, but there was a time, not long ago even, when I was beautiful. Really beautiful. And the fellows were all after me. By the time I was twenty-three I'd lost track of how many proposals I had received. And fun? You can't guess the fun I was having. I traveled everywhere, was sought after as a model, and always the men were around, falling over themselves to get near me. I had the world by the tail. And that was when I made my decision.

"One morning as I was looking at myself in the mirror, I realized that the reason I was having such a full life was because of my beauty. And I decided then that I would never do anything that would detract from or destroy that beauty—and mainly that I would never have children. Having babies was bad for the figure.

"Shortly after that I married, and my husband agreed with my decision. The thoughts of tying ourselves down with children repulsed us both. We wanted to spend our time and money traveling, and on each other. We wanted to be sweethearts, not parents.

"In time, however, we tired of each other and that was when my second husband came along. But it was a short marriage, for he was not the kind of man he pretended to be. That marriage was so short, in fact, that the subject of children never came up.

"I married my third husband when I was almost thirty-four. And believe me, I was even more beautiful then than I was at eighteen."

"Really?" the girl asked. "Gosh, I thought thirty-four was old!"

"Old? Oh my word, no! Fifty isn't even old, young lady.

"My third husband was wealthy and we had a beautiful ranch nestled in the Sierras. He was a good man, and he agreed with me that my intelligence was better served if I wasn't driving kids to school, ballet, or piano lessons."

"But didn't you *want* to be a mother?"

"Oh, I suppose I had motherly instincts, but I satisfied those by raising horses and dogs. My husband and I used to joke about how the animals could never talk back to us the way children do.

"And then one morning just after my forty-fifth birthday my husband was bucked from his horse, broke his neck, died, and I was alone. All alone with horses and dogs."

At that moment the old woman doubled over in pain, and she knew as she lay there in silent agony that it was the worst pain she had ever had. At length, when it subsided, she continued her story, feeling a desperate need to tell it.

"You've no idea, young lady, how lonely I was then . . . and have been ever since, for that matter. I used to ask myself, 'What's going to happen to my life without children? I don't have any focus. What am I living for?' My figure didn't mean as much to me anymore, for no matter what I did, it was spreading out. And it had been years since men had fallen over themselves to be close to me. Suddenly, desperately, I wanted a family.

"Frantically, I began to spend my husband's money searching for another husband—someone who would help me have a child. In the midst of that search I awoke in the middle of one night in excruciating pain. The next day, following exploratory surgery, I learned that I would never have children. That was over ten years ago, and I have been alone ever since, battling this disease without the support of family or friends."

The young girl was silent and the old woman, now feeling the loneliness more keenly than ever before, buried her face and quietly sobbed out her grief.

Not much was said for the rest of the evening, although several times the girl almost spoke, almost shared an idea she had had. It was not until the next morning, however, that she overcame her fear and spoke.

"Ma'am," she said, timidly, "you've got no family and I've got lots. I'll be your family. I'll tell you all the things that a family does, and then you won't be lonely anymore."

And so the days passed quickly with the girl spending endless hours telling the old woman what a real honest-to-goodness family was like.

She had several brothers and sisters, and though only her older brother could come into the hospital to visit, the old woman grew to love them all.

The girl told of her feelings as her younger brothers and sisters were born and of the pain she felt when her baby sister died. She told of successes and of embarrassments, like when her two-year-old brother wandered completely naked down the highway one day. She spoke, too, of arguments they had, but mostly she told of the fun things they did together — working, playing, singing, going places, and just loving each other in every way they could. And the old woman realized one day that the girl's family was a family simply because they loved each other so much. And then she understood that she too had a family.

In the meantime, the girl noticed that the old woman's stomach seizures were becoming less frequent and less severe, and with each day her hope grew that the doctors had been wrong, that her old friend was finally getting better. There was another thing, too, that gave her hope, and that was the obvious sparkle in the old woman's eyes. Daily she seemed happier, her speech was more enthusiastic than ever, and she grew more and more excited to learn about the girl's family.

But there came a night when the girl was awakened by the sounds of hurrying feet, and she opened her eyes only in time to see some nurses and a doctor pushing the old woman's bed out of the door. Through the remainder of the long night she waited, praying and hoping and praying again for her friend.

With dawn, though, a nurse came scurrying into the room pushing an empty bed which she, businesslike, set about making. By noon, when it was still empty, the girl found courage to ask a nurse about the old woman.

"Oh," she replied quietly, "she died last night. Terminal cancer, you know. There was really nothing anybody could do. It's probably better this way, for she was in such great pain. But it is too bad she had to be alone."

For hours the young girl was numb, too grief-stricken even to cry, but at long last her soul began to stir and she began to remember the laughter and tears she and the old woman had shared.

"Love," she thought aloud, surprised. "I love that old woman!"

That afternoon a nurse brought in a letter they had found in the old woman's bedding; a letter addressed simply "Young Lady — Room 117."

"Dear young lady," the letter said, "you'll never know the joy you have brought into my life. Thank you, with all my heart, for sharing your family with me; but most especially, thank you for being my family, my daughter. I am ready to die now, for I know there is someone I leave behind who loves me. I love you, too. I'll see you in heaven."

A Finally Mother

PART TWO

FORCES FROM WITHOUT

As we go through the process of making decisions, we are influenced by a number of variables and factors not of our choosing. Among those factors over which we have little or no control, and yet which seem to exercise such an influence upon us and our decisions, are the experiences of those who have gone before, the attitudes and feelings of those with whom we associate, and the pressures which the world of nature exerts upon us. The following stories reflect decision-making as influenced by these three factors.

ECHO CANYON

There! There was the sound again! A sound that was not so much a sound as it was a whisper, a sigh of something drifting across the snow in the brush below him.

Asel Baldwin shivered and pulled the old buffalo coat more tightly around his shoulders, then tightened his grip on the rifle and squinted into the darkness before him.

"Doggone old fool," he muttered, stomping his feet for warmth as he did so. "I reckon Betsy was right. Again. A sixty-nine-year-old man's got no business here in the snow in Echo Canyon."

She'd told him so, too. Called him a fool even while she was packing up a brace of food to get him into the hills with the rest of the militia. And he'd supposed then she was right. Most of the Nauvoo Legion's Eastern Expedition were young men, and because of his age and his gout, he'd not been asked to go. So why was he here, freezing in a snowstorm on a ledge above Echo Canyon?

The sound came again, and Asel lifted his rifle. But there was nothing to shoot at, and no further noise . . . so cautiously he once again lowered the rifle to his side. Asel knew they were there.

General Wells had warned them that Johnston's Army would send spies, for after Lot Smith's work the entire government outfit was freezing over at Fort Bridger. In fact, just the day before two boys up the trail had captured three army men who claimed to be deserters, but who might be anything, anything at all. So Asel stomped his feet, strained his eyes, and thought with sorrow of Betsy's suffering.

Being sixty-nine and out in the cold was not all that worried Betsy, and old Asel knew it. What really troubled her was that Asel was all she had left, and she dreaded more than anything else being left alone in her old age. Three children she had borne, three fine strapping sons, and now all of them lay dead. Two had died as children, and the third had died at sea. When Asel and Betsy had announced their conversion to Mormonism, their only grown son had stared in shocked silence, turned and picked up his pack, and without a word had walked out of their lives. Two years later they had received word that his ship had gone down, with all hands lost. That had been thirteen years ago, just days before the murder of the Prophet Joseph, and . . .

Wait! He could hear it again, the soft whispering that was more than the sound of snow falling in the darkness. But the wind was playing tricks, and he could not be sure about where . . .

Pushing his rifle before him, he stepped carefully down the hill, straining his tired eyes into the darkness. But the falling snow and the thickness of the scrub oak prevented him from seeing anything clearly.

"Asel," she had wailed, "you'll go and get yourself killed, sure as midnight's dark, you will. Oh, Asel, I just can't bear to be alone!"

"Betsy," he'd replied, trying to calm her. "I'll be fine. There's others there, so I won't be alone. And I've got no choice. I must go. I've told you of my dream of being needed there, and every prayer I've offered since confirms my obligation to go."

"But mine don't," she cried.

"How could the Lord tell you anything, Betsy? Your mind's

already made up. I'm a part of the militia, the prophet has called us into the canyon, and I'm bound to go."

"You old fool," she'd replied angrily. "Go on and get yourself killed, then. Don't care about me! I survived the deaths of our sons. I can surely survive an old fool like you who thinks he's full of revelations about going out into the mountains to get froze or shot full of holes!"

"Betsy . . ."

But she had turned her back, the militia boys were waiting out front, and so with a bitter taste in his mouth and in his heart, Asel Baldwin stomped out the door, certain of the error of his wife's ways. Now though, now he wondered, he surely did. He . . .

The sound came again, the whispering that was almost a part of the wind and yet which wasn't. Asel took two more cautious steps forward, his rifle extended, his heart beating within like a trap-hammer.

"Old fool . . . old fool . . ."

"But Betsy, I need to go . . ."

"Old fool . . ."

The wind died suddenly, and in the utter stillness of the darkened mountain the sound returned, a whispering that Asel knew without doubt was the sound of clothing rubbing through snow and brush.

With his heart pounding wildly and his breath coming in ragged gasps, old Asel placed one frozen foot before the other and moved toward the oak brush, certain now that the sound had come from there. Twice he checked the cap on his rifle, knowing full well that it was there and that the powder, lead, and wadding were in place and tamped down. Yet still he checked it, needing the security it gave him. Another step, then another, and a gust of wind kicked against him, skittering snow before it and rattling the few dry oak leaves that were left in the brush. Asel, startled, jerked his rifle to his shoulder and spun in a half-circle, his heart in his throat. But there was nothing, nothing but the brush, the snow, and the darkness.

"Old fool . . . old . . ."

Asel shook his head, trying to drive away his wife's words, trying to recall the positive feelings he had experienced after he had laid the matter before the Lord. But it was no use. He was too cold and too frightened and too old. Betsy was right. He had no business being in the mountains guarding against Johnston's Army. Tomorrow he would . . .

Again the faint sound of clothing rubbing against something assailed his ears, and Asel, courageous in spite of his knowledge of the ultimate result of his moving forward, stepped into the edge of the brush. With all the power of his being he strained his eyes and his ears, ignoring the cold sweat on his body and the pounding in his chest, trying to determine where the sound was coming from.

He took another cautious step and paused, listening. Then he took three more and again stopped. His eyes probed into the darkness, looking through the spectral trunks of the trees, past the rock, down the . . .

The rock?

Asel's old heart once more leaped into his throat, for he suddenly remembered that in the daylight there had been no rock there. He knew, for he had memorized every feature of the hill.

With a prayer in his heart that God would take care of Betsy, Asel stepped around a clump of brush and into clear view of the man crouched in the snow. As he did so there was a click, a flash, and a sudden explosion, and Asel felt his buffalo coat jerk violently back against his body.

"Old fool . . ."

With startling clarity, Asel realized that his own rifle was at his shoulder and aimed, and that his finger was tightening on the trigger . . .

"Old fool . . ."

"So, ma, that's how it was. Pa didn't shoot, and when he realized that my bullet had only hit his coat he walked over to me and we both recognized each other at the same time. I was rescued in the Caribbean, joined the army, deserted to come find you folks, got hurt in a fall, and well . . . if pa hadn't been there . . ."

"Billy, I called your pa an old fool, while all along the name should have been mine. But praise God that Asel was in tune. I'm so thankful you're finally home."

"Me too, ma. Me too."

OLD ZION

The sharpness of the sun's heat was dulled by the smooth blue haze that spread over the valley. Indian summer it was called. Old Zion knew that the blue smoke was supposed to be coming from the Indians' fires as they roasted their corn, nuts and fish for the winter ahead. But the Indians were long since gone, the smoke still came, and Zion wondered if they shouldn't change the name. The quietness of the afternoon was disturbed only by the slow rythmic thumping of the mended rocker as Old Zion rocked untiringly back and forth. The porch upon which he sat had originally been made of rough lumber, but the weathering of many years and many feet had worn it to a shiny smoothness, much like the backs of his wife's hands.

Zion looked at her as she sat quietly in her wicker chair, slowly moving the bamboo fan in front of her face. Even after all these years his Amelia was still beautiful. How, he wondered, had he ever persuaded her to marry him?

Zion was a taciturn man, not given to much speech. Occasionally he would get started talking, however, and then his deep heavy voice would enchant and enthrall everyone who listened. He loved to tell stories, and his listeners, bound under his spell, were always sorry when he stopped. He was a short man, and his thick shoulders and chest told a story of many years of hard work. His eyes, however, were what people noticed most about him. They were black, unusually large, and very bright, like the surface of a mountain lake glittering in the moonlight. He was also an Indian.

The shrill ki-yi-yi of a young pup pierced the peaceful air, and in a moment the animal came scampering over the hill, a young boy running breathlessly beside him.

"Zion," the boy panted when the pair had reached the porch, "Shep tangled with a porcupine and I don't know what to do and . . ."

"Whoa up, son, or you'll die from lack of breath. Bring the pup here, and we'll take care of him."

"Zion's sharp knife had soon cut the tip off each of the quills that filled the dog's nose, and with the gas expelled, they were easy to pull out. Still whimpering, but seeming to know that everything was going to be all right, the dog expressed his thanks by licking the old man's hand as he lay cuddled in his lap.

The boy had only just disappeared when Breck Jensen (so called because he so enjoyed breakfast) walked up to the porch.

"Zion, my milch cow vanished during the night, and I been all day tryin' to fetch her back. But you know me. I can't follow signs for sour apples. Suppose you could saddle up and come help me find her?"

"Oh, I reckon so. Let me feed the sheep, and I'll be with you."

"Thanks, Zion. I'll meet you up by the Swedish temple. I followed her sign to there."

"Zion," his wife said admiringly as Breck rode off, "your birthright has given you many talents. Folks hereabouts certainly have a lot of respect for you."

Old Zion looked over at Amelia, his heart going out to her. Cataracts had long since pulled the shades of darkness over her vision, and now he was her sight every bit as much as she was his life. He couldn't imagine how he could ever get along without her. He held her hand as he helped her into the house so she could begin supper, and his heart skipped, but only one beat. After all, he thought grinning, he *was* nearly eighty!

As Zion kindled the fire in the old Majestic range he thought of what Amelia had said. "Amelia," he spoke slowly, as he slid the kerosene can back out of the way behind the stove, "folks may respect me some now, but there was a time when that just wasn't so."

Amelia didn't answer for there was no need to. She knew far too well the old hurts and pains of which her husband spoke. Many of them she had experienced herself, and they had talked the others over so thoroughly that Zion knew her mind well regarding them. She knew, in spite of her blindness, that he didn't expect an answer. He was only talking to himself.

As Zion walked away from the little house, crossed the creek and climbed the rocky trail to tend his small band of sheep, his thoughts returned to the birthright Amelia had spoken of. And as he climbed, each step took him farther back into his memories.

Chief Siegnerouch had given the order. "He is to die!" And though the boy was hardly past the crawling stage, he had been tied securely to a tree and a large pile of dried wood had been placed around him ready for burning.

"Hold it," a man had called from a passing wagon. "What goes on here?"

Chief Siegnerouch, very young himself, had tried to explain to the man that the child's mother was dead, his father was away on a scouting trip, the boy cried too loud and too much, no one wanted to take care of him, and so he had to die.

After much haggling the chief and the immigrant agreed upon a purchase price for the boy: nine bushels of wheat, one sack of flour and a heifer calf. And so it was that to this young Mormon couple from England, George and Emma Brown, a son was "born" on April 12, 1855. Because the Browns had no children of their own, they were especially thrilled over this little boy that had come to them in America, and so it seemed only right that his name should be Zion.

During his life Old Zion had felt both pride and shame because of his Indian heritage, but as a youth he had felt mostly shame. In fact, during those years he would have done anything to become white. It was also during his youth that the Mormon settlements were under almost constant pressure from Indian attacks. To make matters worse, whenever a group of men went into the mountains to cut timber for their homes or for the new meetinghouse they were building, or if the town herders would take their livestock into a new area, the Indians always seemed to know about it. They would then strike quickly, gaining whatever advantage they could over the settlers. Many times, because Zion was Indian, he was called before the elders to try to prove his innocence on the charge of spying.

"Who have you talked with outside the fort?" someone would snap.

"Nobody. I ain't bin outside!"

"Then how did you get the word out to them?"

"I didn't!"

"Someone is telling the Indians our plans, and we think it is you. Now tell us how you did it."

Zion, then as now, did not talk easily. He was by nature secretive, and when he said anything at all he found himself wondering how much good it did. But that time, like so many others, it was Bishop Johnson who came to his rescue.

"Zion," he asked, "are you telling us the truth?"

"Yes," Zion replied quietly.

"My boy Luke plays with Zion and he says he is honest," said Bishop Johnson. "That is good enough for me."

He remembered that there had been some reluctance about dismissing him that easily, but after several threats and words of warning he had been set free.

As Old Zion forked hay over the fence to the sheep he recalled his feelings that day, and his determination to prove to them that he was trustworthy. That chance had come on a warm spring day about a week later.

Luke Johnson and he liked to explore, and that day they wanted to examine the mysteries of a high peak overlooking the valley, a hill called Devil's Lookout. It was rightly named, for every so often the devilish redmen would post sentries on the hill to observe the actions of the settlers below.

Zion and Luke had worked their way up through the brush of the lower slope, leaving markers where they had left snares along rabbit trails, until they reached the base of the rimrock. As they looked for a way up through the cliff, a small patch of cedars just below them exploded and a large buck deer plunged out of its hiding place. Looking all legs and horns it sent rocks and dead branches flying in all directions as it lunged for seclusion around the hill. The two boys, their hearts thumping wildly, stared after it in silence long after it had disappeared. Wondering then if there might be another, they settled themselves comfortably under an overhang where they could observe the hill and the entire valley below.

Luke heard the hoofbeats first, and in terror he grasped Zion's arm and pushed him farther under the ledge, at the same time motioning for silence. The steady rhythm of horse's hooves striking on rock stopped directly above them. The language and the voices quickly told the boys that the intruders were Indians, or at least all but one of them was. Then Zion heard the name *Siegnerouch,* and his heart stopped as though an arrow had pierced it. Siegnerouch? He who had almost put him to death? Here?

Pressed as tightly as they could press into the crevice at the foot of the ledge, breathing shallowly and praying fervently that their thumping hearts would not reveal their presence, the two boys listened carefully to the conversation. Whose was that voice? To whom did it belong?

To Zion, past experiences seemed to return in unexplainable bursts of memory, very brief but very distinct. He was back in the bishop's home facing the elders. "Someone is telling the Indians our plans, and we think it is you." And then, as though a giant puzzle were tumbling its many parts back into place, he recognized the voice. It was one of the elders at the meeting.

After what seemed forever the horses pulled back, a lone rider rode off down the hill toward the fort, and the sound of the Indians' horses disappeared. Inching their clammy bodies from the crack in the rock, the two boys felt lucky just to be alive. After a whispered conference the boys fled down the hill, not even pausing to check their snares, and in a short time they were standing in Bishop Johnson's home.

After listening to their account the bishop sat silent for some time, deep in thought. Then he stood and walked over to the boys, placed his arms around each of them, and held them close.

"Thank you, boys. Because of your courage and strength we now have a few hours in which to get ready. May God bless you both."

As Old Zion closed and tied the gate securely and then turned back toward his home, he recalled how Bishop Johnson's face had seemed to shine when he had smiled at him. His eyes glistening, the bishop had taken Zion's hand in his and squeezed it.

"Zion," he'd said, "when this is all over, you will never have to prove yourself again. From this day forward, walk with your head erect. The day will come when all about you will admire you, and will seek your wisdom and help."

Gingerly, Old Zion climbed into his tack shed, lifted his saddle and bridle, and started toward his horse. It was time, he thought, that he go find Breck Jensen's cow.

THE HIGH PLACE

The young man stood beneath the shade of the juniper, staring upward at the sheer face of the cliff. It reared its head above him, stretching nearly a thousand feet upward, to end in a sharp point that the old ones had called The High Place. The hill had once been considered sacred, he knew, and this was actually the first time he had ever been this close to it. But today was the day upon which he had determined to become a man, today he would ascend the cliff.

He had watched that cliff all his life, fearing it from the day when he first realized that one day he must climb it. It wasn't so much the climbing that would make a man of him, he understood that. It was something unknown, something that would occur on The High Place, which would bring about that result.

Of his people, there were but few who had climbed it, and those who had done so refused to say much about it. Yet he and the others respected them tremendously, and more than all else he wished for the same kind of respect that was shown them. Then too, those who had climbed it experienced a change, somehow, and he desperately wanted that change in his life.

He thought of his parents, with whom he argued a great deal lately. He knew they loved him, for such was the way of his people, and he guessed he loved them also, but for some reason they could not get along with each other any longer.

The young man understood the problem very well; his parents were simply overprotective. They refused to trust his judgment, to allow him to make decisions on his own. They still thought of him as a child, little more than a baby, who could not be allowed to make his own way in the world.

It was like climbing this cliff. For years his parents had known he would one day do it, and both had worried themselves sick over it. His mother had pleaded that he not make the attempt, or if he must, to seek counsel from his father before trying. His father, never really against his climbing the cliff, had adamantly insisted that when the young man decided to try, he involve his father in the climb. What a pathetic idea that was! He needed to do it on his own to gain the respect he so badly wanted. If his people found out his father had helped, they'd laugh him silly. There was no way he would allow that to happen.

So this morning he had crept from the house when his parents and little brothers and sister still slept, had totally fooled them, and now he was ready to begin the ascent.

Smiling as he thought of what his friends would say when they learned of his accomplishment, he began climbing. At first it was not so bad, but then the sun appeared, and before long he was perspiring heavily. It also grew increasingly dangerous, and his pace grew slower by the hour. Before long his hands were torn and bloody, and so were his knees. From one handhold or toehold to another he inched his way upward, nearly falling several times and yet always managing, just barely, to cling to the face of the cliff. At one point, for a hundred feet or so, he had easy going, for he found a chimney or crack in the face of the cliff through which he climbed. At another place he found a narrow ledge that wound its way upward for a short distance, and along that he simply walked. But those were the only easy places, and the remainder of the climb was a dangerous and grueling torture.

It was late afternoon when the young man, exhausted, bloody, and filled with terror at the thoughts of the descent still before him, finally dragged his battered body over the lip of the cliff to lie spent on the smoothly worn stone of The High Place. He had made it, he knew, but he also knew that he would spend the night there and would likely die the next day trying to get down. He was simply not capable of that climb.

At last he crawled to the edge and stared downward into the dizzying depths, and as he did, he no longer thought of the praise of his friends or of the honor, respect and glory his people would show him. He thought only of his parents and family, and of what his death would do to them.

Why oh why hadn't he asked his father for help, for advice? Bitterly he cursed himself, and then tears stained his cheeks as he wept openly, his grief a combination of fear, self-pity, and genuine concern for his family.

For a long time he lay thus, but at length, his emotions spent, he rose to his knees to move back to the center of The High Place. But he couldn't move! He was so filled with terror that his legs refused to operate, and so at last he had to worm his way back to the center.

As he worked his way around, trying to get as comfortable as possible, he began to think about his accomplishment, and for the first time he realized how proud he was that he had stood on The High Place. Not many could say that, he knew, and at least, should he die tomorrow, he would be remembered as a hero, he who had climbed the . . .

A flash of white under the edge of a nearby rock caught his attention, and the young man wormed his way to it. It was a torn piece of paper, and as he unfolded it he wondered what great message some previous visitor had left him. At last, hands shaking, he opened the paper, and as he read he felt the change that would take him from boyhood to true manhood. The note said simply:

Dear Son,

When we awoke this morning and found you gone, I came immediately to The High Place to await your arrival. But you have taken so long that your little sister, who came with me, needed to get home. So we have started back. If you had only asked me this morning, I could have told you of the steps the Old Ones carved on the south end of the cliff. That would have saved you all the grief and agony, and most of the day as well.

My son, the true test of manhood is not that you have climbed to The High Place. Anyone can do that. The true test is how you did it. When a man is humble enough to involve those around him in his climbs, then he is a man.

Now hurry down the trail. We'll be going slow, waiting for you.

Love,
Your Father

SIGNALS

July 29, 1925
Sanpete County, Utah

I had a rough night last night. Coyotes got three sheep. I should've known, as I heard the commotion through my sleep. I know it's no excuse, but I was just too tired to come awake. The rain and lightning storm yesterday scattered the herd pretty thoroughly, and I was till long after dark getting them gathered and the bunch back onto North Flat. Then my tent was washed out and a good many supplies were soaked and ruined, and it was way past midnight before I finally got to sleep. So I was exhausted, and that cost me the sheep.

I didn't get the big fire lit for the same reason. The wood was too wet to burn easily, and by the time I got around to trying I was too dad-burned beat to fight with it. So my family didn't get their signal last night, either. Like I said, it was a rough night.

For breakfast this morning I had coyote-killed mutton and sourdough flapjacks, and that and beans will be my menu until week after next, when my boys bring up the supplies. I'd like to have 'em come up sooner, but there's no way I can contact them and

certainly no way I can leave the herd to go myself. I wonder sometimes at the irony of sitting here on the mountain, with home in
such plain sight down in the valley, and feeling that I'm so far
away, almost in another world.

After breakfast I moved the herd south into the top of Pole
Canyon and pitched the tent high on the steep slope. The pines are
above and to the south of me, except of course in Gammet, which
is directly to the north. But here on the shelf there is a fine copse
of aspen, some large boulders down where the hill drops off steep,
and a good view of town below me in the valley.

Once I got the sheep settled I took out my knife, worked a new
edge onto it, and spent a couple of hours finishing a little chair and
doll for Victora. I miss her — her and the boys. Victora is fast
becoming a young lady now — seems like each time I go home
she's grown six inches. She's filling out faster than I would like, and
she is becoming much more gentle. Knowing that, I suppose these
little dolls are not the things she'd be most excited about. But I
don't know what else to do for her. I'm not much of a hand with
words, out loud that is. So I do my talking with my knife, making
little dolls, chains, cages with balls in 'em, and so on. I don't reckon
my children really understand me yet. But God willing one day
they will know how much each of them means to me, and how I'm
trying to tell them so with what I make for them.

ValGene is rapidly becoming a fine man. He's tall and quiet and
we hardly ever have to tell him what to do anymore. He sees it
and does it himself. He also watches out for the younger kids, and
he takes special care of Victora. When I'm at the herd he's the one
who has to take care of the family.

Delbert I worry a little about. He's as hard a worker as I've
seen, nearly as tall as ValGene, and every whit as headstrong as his
grandpa was. He does about what he wants, about when he wants
to do it, and neither his ma nor I have much to say about it anymore. But I'm not really worried — Delbert knows people, and he
truly cares about them. With that quality I expect great things from
him.

Victora is next, and besides what I've already said, what more is there? Only a man who has a daughter will ever understand how I feel about that little girl.

Gayle is almost nine now, just got baptized this past fall, and is always into some adventure or another. But he's a sober boy too, always does what he's asked. We have him caring for the goats and bummer lambs; he takes his turn milking; and last time the supplies were brought up, he helped. He wants a horse, so this fall I'll see what I can find for him. Seems to me that Gayle is a natural leader —that comes from their grandpa too. Last fall when Gayle was confirmed he was told in his blessing that his life was the Lord's. Knowing Gayle, that makes sense to me. Because of that he'll likely have some rough times, but he'll grow from them. We all do.

Forest is five and as full of the Old Nick as any five-year-old I've ever seen. He has an imagination longer than my arm, and he keeps all of us going with his tales. But he sure loves his brothers. Nellie told me last time I was down that his greatest hope in the whole world is to be a sheepherder like his pa. That's fine for now, I suppose, but I hope he'll move on to better things. Not that I'm ashamed of what I'm doing, of course, but it sure is tough trying to be a husband and a father when I'm only home two or three weeks out of the year. Forest will have a choice about what he does; I don't suppose I ever did. I had no education to speak of, and all I've ever known is livestock. Still, some of the sheep here are my own, I make a living for my family, and what more can a man ask for? The occupation is honorable, and I've always tried to do my best at it. A little while ago I carved my brand, the quarter-circle Y, my initials, HVY, and the date on a quakie here by the tent. It's foolish, I suppose, to carve up a tree like that. But I've honored both my name and the brand which represents it for as long as I can remember, and I'm proud of that. Maybe some day my children or their children will see what I carved and feel the same kind of pride in our name that I do. I hope so.

The lightning yesterday put me in mind of Nellie, and I've been sitting here for some time watching the town and thinking of her.

I've never known anyone who was so terrified of storms as she is. I don't feel that way, but maybe if I'd gone through what she went through as a girl I'd feel the same. So yesterday when all the lightning was flashing I was thinking of her, wishing I was there to hold her and tell her that she didn't need to worry about any storms.

Missing her is the worst part of this business, and there are days when I practically have to tie myself to a tree to keep from heading on down to see her. I don't know for certain, but I think she feels as lonely as I do. Sometimes we both come close to saying it, but mostly it goes unsaid. Her eyes, though—when I'm home I like to watch her eyes—that's how I know how she feels. If only I could find a way to tell her how I feel, to tell her how much she means to me, to tell her how terrible much I love her. But the mountains and the desert put their silence on a man, and the more time I spend in the solitude of these hills the more like them I become. Words mostly don't mean much up here. So instead of talking or writing I carve, hoping Nellie and the kids will one day understand.

I think too of our children who died, though less often, I suppose, than I should. Little Ray was alive and kicking until moments before he was born. Might have been my fault that he died. I was the only one to help Nellie in the birth, and my hands are rough and unskilled. If I had known more, could I have done something? Oh, dear God, if it was my fault, please forgive me. I'd do anything to get him back!

Martha too. Her death was harder on Nellie than me, coming nine days after her birth. But still it was pretty tough for both of us. Nellie sat and rocked that lifeless little body all night, sobbing quietly in the dark. What could I have said to her? When I need the words, why don't they ever come? I recall the next morning, Lord. I tried to explain to Nellie that before the children became ours they were yours, and that gave you the right to do as you pleased with them. Why couldn't I explain that to her? Wouldn't that have helped ease her pain? And shouldn't that be something that a husband ought to do? Why can't I ever say what I feel? All I can do is care for livestock and whittle. Talk about a couple of useless talents. I'd surely like to know, Lord, what you had in mind when you made me.

Well, I'd better put this aside so I can go gather up some wood for my fire. This shelf is a good place for it, in sight of most of the town. I'm sitting up here where my family will see the fire easily. They know I'm here someplace, but they're not certain just where. The fire will change that, and then for a few moments they'll watch and know what I'm saying even though no words will be spoken.

Lord, I just thought of something. Isn't that a whole lot like you do things? While we can't see you, you see us clearly, and every so often you build a fire to let us know you're still there and still thinking of us. Some of those fires are called miracles, some are called revelations, and some are called good feelings and burnings in our hearts. Makes no matter what you call them, they're still fires, still signals.

Lord, when my family sees my signal fire tonight, help them to know they're filling my thoughts and heart. Help them to understand that I love them more than I can tell them with words, like I feel, Lord, when I see your fires and get your signals. Help Nellie to know how much she means to me, and how I ache for the ability to tell her so. Finally, Lord, help my family to one day be able to read my journal — the letters I've written to them with my knife in these little pieces of wood. Like this one, Lord; this little armchair. I've spent all afternoon on it, thinking all these thoughts into it. A little chair like this isn't worth anything, unless one day one of my family can understand the thoughts I've had while carving it.

Well, since I didn't get a fire built last night, tonight I'd better build one twice as big as usual. That way, Nellie and the kids will know I'm all right. Lord, I'd be mighty grateful if you could build a little fire too. I think, like my family, I also need a signal tonight.

THE LIZZIE PROJECT

Sunshine, hot on my back, was raising a tiny river of sweat which trickled down between my shoulder blades, causing me to squirm uncomfortably. Where I was standing, leaning against the old porch rail, I was square in the sun. I was also almost directly in front of the man everyone called Crazyman Mose. And that made me as uncomfortable as the sun did.

I was just a green kid then, maybe fifteen. But summer was newly arrived, and like all kids just out of school I was alive with the excitement of adventure sure to come. Other summers had brought other experiences, both good and bad, but this one, we had vowed, would be the best yet. For this summer, if our dreams came true, we would have us a car, a real car.

Out of the corners of my eyes I looked at my buddies. Whiffles and the Spinner were squatted against the rail to my left, Tobe was holding up the sagging pillar of the porch to my right, and it didn't take too much concentration to see that all of them were as uncomfortable as I was. And none of us was saying anything, either. Once, way off, I heard a dog barking, and once a rooster, strutting around out in the yard, got mad at some chicken and took off after her. But other than that the only sounds I could hear were made by the old man who sat leaning back in his rickety chair against the door frame.

I had no idea how old he was, but if I'd had to guess I would have said he was anywhere between ninety and three hundred and ten, with his true age probably coming closer to the last figure. On the top of his wrinkled old head there was very little hair, just a gray suggestion that once there had been something there. On his chin, though, there was considerably more. I don't think he'd shaved since the last time he'd been to church, which was maybe sixty years before, and his beard, gray and straggly, snarled its way down onto his old bib overalls.

Like I said, he wasn't saying any more than the rest of us, but that doesn't mean his mouth wasn't working. It was going like a regular clock, chewing away on the black quid that kept oozing out from the corner of his mouth to trickle down his chin and finally disappear into the single dark area of his beard, which of course kept getting darker the more he chewed.

I shifted a little, feeling worse than awful, and I could see that the other guys were just as nervous as I was, and about as anxious to be gone. After all, it was a pretty tough way to spend a perfectly good Saturday afternoon, sitting around on Crazyman Mose's porch, watching him chew tobacco. Still, we had an idea, and if anything was to come of it we had this to do, like it or not. So we sat, knowing that when he was ready he would talk, and until then we wouldn't hear a word.

Having nowhere else to go, my thoughts drifted off and wandered up one of the bony and serrated ridges of the nearby mountain. My eyes followed my thoughts, climbing upward to finally come to rest on the blackness of a stand of high-up timber. For a moment I thought how cool it would be in those pines, and I could almost hear the wind as it sighed through their boughs. What I wouldn't give to be there, I thought wistfully. Where I stood on the porch it was hot enough to sunburn a horned toad, and I was getting more miserable by the minute.

The droning of a fly in the shade of the porch brought my attention back to the present, and after a second or two I located the tiny creature hovering in the air between me and the old man. Squinting one eye I tried to line it up with the wart on the old man's nose, but I'd just about get him there and the fly would move. In a minute, though, it came back and I tried it again. Suddenly, however, it left the porch and darted in the doorway to land on the handle of the poker which was leaning against the stove.

I was still watching it when I became aware that the old man was coming slowly down onto all four legs of his chair. My buddies and I stared transfixed as he slowly leaned forward, his head swiveling toward the doorway, the movement of his mouth increasing in tempo.

For perhaps fifteen seconds I held my breath as the old man studied the fly. Then with a slight jerk of his head a black stream issued from between his teeth and arched through the air to splat against the hot stove not half an inch from where the insect was perched. The fly was instantly gone, and we all watched spellbound as the tobacco juice sizzled slowly down the side of the stove.

Inwardly I shuddered with revulsion. If I had never made up my mind before about whether or not to try tobacco, I certainly had just then.

Slowly the old man straightened up, his mouth working again, and for the first time I noticed his yellow teeth, what few of them there were left. Another indictment against tobacco. The case was getting stronger by the minute. I really didn't like this old man.

"Ah'll be goin' to a hot place," he swore to no one in particular. "Third miss today. Must be slippin'!"

And when he said that I couldn't help but grin, for I was instantly reminded of something that mom always said. She said that wherever you found one sin, if you'd just wait a bit you'd surely find one or two others to go along with it. Most sins travel in company, and do hate to be alone. It was purely amazing how many times my folks were right.

"So you fellers are wondering about my Lizzie," he suddenly croaked. "Well, what in thunder is it you want to know?"

There was a general shuffling on all sides of me, and I was aware that my three so-called friends were waiting for me. Why on earth, I groaned, couldn't I have good luck for a change? How come whenever we pitched rocks or drew straws or whatever we did to see who got the raw end of some kind of deal, it was always me who ended up in that shiny spot? I'll tell you, in some things there's absolutely no justice in life. None at all.

Scrud, I didn't have anything to say to this crazy dirty old man! No sir I didn't! I didn't even want to be here. I'd voted against it. Why . . .

For some reason I made the mistake of looking over at Whiffles, and the look on his face told me I'd better have something to say. I'd also better have it to say pretty darn quick or he'd have plenty to say to me later. Now I'd seen Whiffles at work in that department before, and I knew there was nothing I wanted him to say to me. Not that way! So I cleared my throat once or twice and set out on my lonesome journey.

"Ah . . . ah . . . umph, er, ah . . . Craz . . er . . Mr. Mose . . ."

"Jensen, boy," the old man croaked. "Name's Moses Jensen, and I ain't crazy, like you was about to say. Sometimes I get to thinkin' that some of the folks who come around might be, but I sure enough ain't! Well, go ahead, speak it out. What is it you want?"

"Uh . . . Mr. Jensen, er . . . about that old car out there in your alfalfa field . . .?"

"That there is Lizzie, boy. Her name is Lizzie! So what about her? Speak up!"

Desperately I looked over at Tobe and the Spinner, mentally pleading for their help. But they were staring at the cracks in the porch, studiously avoiding even the smallest hint that they might somehow be associated with me. I swiveled my glance to Whiffles, and the look he gave me would make an icicle feel feverish. Some friends!

With an effort I looked again at the old man, clearing my throat once more while I tried to think of some good way to ask the question.

"Ah, Mr. Jensen, sir. We . . . ah . . ."

"Spit it out, boy! Spit it out. You're being timed with a watch, not a calendar. At the rate you're talkin' I could die of old age before you're half through."

Well, I was about to agree with him when I heard my buddies start in to snickering, and that got my mad up. Those guys weren't going to laugh at me! Throwing back my shoulders and putting as tough a look on my face as I could, I glowered back at the old man, trading frown for frown. The snickering stopped instantly, and then I upped and asked him could we have the old Model A Ford which was rusting away out in his alfalfa field.

I know the question was sudden, but I surely didn't expect what happened next. Old Mr. Jensen didn't say anything, he just started huffing and puffing, getting louder by the minute, and then he started in to cussing, letting out a string of words that would have sizzled the grass for yards around, had there been any to sizzle. I thought sure he was going to come after me, and I was all set to run. But he didn't. He just came to a high boil and then simmered off, and he never even got out of his rickety old chair. He just sat there and let the steam come out.

Me, I stood there watching him and that got me to thinking, and the more I thought the more upset at my buddies I got. I knew that old man would never go along with our crazy idea. I'd told the guys so. It was dumb as a bedbug asking somebody to give you their car. It was dumb even if the car was an old wrecked Model A Ford like his, sitting unused for years in the middle of a field. That made no matter. A car was a car, and you got a car by buying it, not just up and asking for it. Good grief!

"We didn't mean to upset you," I said quickly. "We were just looking for an opportunity . . ."

"It has found you," he growled suddenly. "Sort of. For years I've wanted to get that outfit running. This may be the time. What names do you go by?"

I told him, still not sure whether he had said what it sounded to me like he had said.

"So you young whippersnappers figure on getting Lizzie to run, do you?" He paused, doing his best to grin, and I noticed again how many gaps there were in his teeth.

"You got a license?"

Tobe nodded in the affirmative, and I saw that he was fingering the fishing license pinned to his hat. Well, it was a license, all right. I had to give Tobe credit for that.

"Shucks," the old man said. "I've always wanted to see Lizzie cutting figures down the road again. She was a right purty outfit in her day, I'd tell a man! As I recollect, she run when I parked her there in the field. I was always going to start her up, but one thing led to another and I just never got around to it. Then of a sudden I was about too old anyway, so here I sit and there she sits.

"Why, pshaw," he said, spitting at one of his chickens. "It'd be right fine if somebody got one or the other of us to running again. You young fellers reckon you can do it, get Lizzie started, I mean?"

I got my surprised mouth open to answer him, but before I could say anything Whiffles and the Spinner took over. I figured then that I was only to be the spokesman until the dirty work was over. Which it seemed it now was. But that was okay considering the outcome, for now we had us a car, and in my mind's eye I could already see us, motoring down main street, the four of us together, waving to everybody with that little one-finger-over-the-steering-wheel wave, and being admired by all who saw us. I'll tell you, having a car was one fine thing.

"It's all set, then?" Whiffles finally asked. "We can have it?"

"Not by a long shot, you can't," the old man growled. "I said you could fix Lizzie. I didn't say you could have her. She's mine! Always has been . . . will be 'til I push up daisies. She's my friend."

"You mean . . ."

"That's right, sonny. You fix her for the practice. Period. Maybe I let you use her a couple of times . . . we'll see. Depends on how hard you work and if one of you gets hisself a real license, not one to go fishin' with."

Well, I was surprised. This old man, dirty as he was, had maybe more on the ball than any of us had supposed. It was not going to be easy getting us a car. Still, that old Model A was our best prospect and we all knew it, so we looked at each other, nodded, and the deal was made. The Lizzie project was started. We would fix the old man's car, and just maybe he would let us drive it once or twice when it was done. How wonderful! Scrud!

As soon as we could tear ourselves away from Mr. Jensen we sprinted the half block to where the old car sat, scattering chickens and little porkers all along the way. Thing is, I don't know why we were hurrying. That old car was going nowhere — fast. Just like us. We found all four tires flat; the rubber looked rotten; when we lifted up one side of the hood to look at the engine we found a petrified pack rat nest and a very active wasp colony; there weren't any seats left to speak of; and we were beginning to wonder what we'd gotten into.

Whiffles had told old Mr. Jensen that each of us knew pretty much what we were doing, mechanically speaking, and I suppose that was true. Pretty much.

Whiffles could usually keep his dad's tractor running, Tobe and the Spinner fiddled around with their dads' pickups all the time, and yours truly had finally gotten to where he could unjam the hay baler when it got stuck. So you can see that we were all experts at one thing or another. Pretty much.

Still, this was looking more and more like a mighty large project, so we climbed into the old outfit to talk things over. That was when we discovered the red ant bed in the floorboards. From then on we sat out in the alfalfa when we talked.

"First off," the Spinner said after we'd stopped tooting each other's horns, "we've got to have us a plan — some way of making that crazy old fogey give us his car."

"Maybe he'll die," Tobe said, in a hopeful voice.

"Fat chance," Whiffles replied. "He's too dang ornery to die. Nope, there's got to be another way, a way where we'll be in control."

It took us about an hour batting ideas around before Whiffles hit a home run clear out of the alfalfa patch. The idea was a beaut, too, so simple and yet so great.

When it came time to try and start Lizzie, we'd bring a can half filled with gas, put a little on the car and none in it, and then act like it was full while we tried to get it to run. After a while, when it didn't, the old man was sure to get discouraged enough that, if asked just right, he'd want to give the car to us, just to get rid of it himself. Only problem was, it was kind of dishonest. That bothered all of us a little, but after we thought about it we decided that the car wasn't really his anyway. He'd given up the right to it when he'd parked it and left it all those years ago. Besides, if we were going to put all our money and time into it, then by rights it ought to be ours, not his. Our plan was simply to get *our* car into *our* ownership. It was that simple.

"Boys," Whiffles smiled, getting up. "Now that we've figured out how to get the car, let's start figuring out how to get her started."

Beginning that afternoon it seemed like we worked on Lizzie every spare minute of our lives, and some not-so-spare minutes, too. There were a couple of times, in fact, when I thought my dad was going to inflict great bodily harm, but I escaped, and it all worked out. We jacked Lizzie up on blocks and took all the tires off and had them repaired down at the garage (you should have heard the comments there!); we worked the engine over as thoroughly as we knew how, both inside and out; we scrubbed down the inside of the car with lye soap given us by an obliging grandmother (let me tell you, *that* stuff got rid of the ants *and* most of the skin on our hands, too); we oiled and greased everything we could possibly oil and grease, including ourselves; and we sat around for three days waiting for one of Mr. Jensen's geese, penned up for obvious reasons, to get rid of five nuts and bolts he had eaten with obvious relish.

And all this time old Mr. Jensen was a real pain in the neck. He hovered around every minute that he could, feeling naturally interested in what we were doing. That part wasn't so bad. But he wanted to help, and that was where it got rough. He was too old to hold on to any tools, so he spent the time leaning on his cane spitting tobacco at his geese and giving us useless directions.

"Tighten that whatchamacallit," he'd holler! "Loosen that there thingamajig, you young whippersnappers! Put that doohickey there with that thingamabob outfit, and Lizzie'll be runnin' in no time flat!"

At first we laughed at his ignorance, remembering what we were putting over on him. But time and grease and sore knuckles wore down our patience, and soon the old man was a downright irritating nuisance. There were times when it was all I could do to keep from yelling at him, but the other guys held me back and I was able to keep it all inside. Still, it sure would have been easier if he had just died, either that or stayed home. Most days I wouldn't have cared which.

What was strange, though, was that after a few days it seemed as though Mr. Jensen had started liking us. Occasionally, he was waiting at the car when we got there, and if he wasn't there he arrived soon after we did. He also started talking sometimes, not yelling, telling us of places he had gone in the Lizzie and of things he had seen. He especially liked Whiffles and the Spinner, with Tobe in third place and me somewhere out on an iceberg. Naturally I returned his sentiments.

We learned he had no family—his wife and only son were already dead—and so obviously he was lonely. I suppose that was why he took to us like he did. In fact, after a couple of weeks he had become downright sociable.

We kept hoping, as we built up our friendship with him, that he would on his own give us the car. That would have saved us a lot of trouble. But he didn't, even after about a ton of hints from all of us. So there was no choice, finally, but to go ahead with our plans.

At last the day came when we figured we were ready to start the Lizzie. While the Spinner went to get the old man, Whiffles put in the crank, Tobe advanced the spark, and I began to grunt and sweat. For an hour or so we groaned in heavy labor, but the old car didn't even so much as cough. In fact, it did nothing, nothing at all. It just sat there — thank goodness!

At last, exhausted, we sprawled out in the alfalfa to rest and recuperate, vocally expressing to each other some of the thoughts of our hearts.

"Was I you fellers," advised the old man, "I'd give Lizzie a little incentive."

We all groaned and rolled over, wondering to ourselves what great pearl of wisdom Mr. Jensen would come up with this time.

"What do you mean, an incentive?" Tobe asked, for once getting his words out faster than Whiffles or the Spinner.

"Just what I said, boy. Lizzie there is particular, and she's got to have a reason for going. It's been so long since she run that she can't hardly remember what it was like, or how much fun it was. Was I you, I'd put her in gear and then give her a push, just to sort of remind her. Seems like that's what it used to take, so I reckon it ought to work now. Give it a try."

"Push it?" Tobe groaned, echoing my thoughts exactly. "I'm so beat now I can't even walk, let alone push this old hunk of junk!"

"Me too," agreed the Spinner. "If this heap was gonna run it would have done it by now. We've gassed it up, we've done everything else we can think of to do. It won't get any more compression by pushing than we gave it with the crank. I say let's forget the whole deal."

Well, besides being impressed with the Spinner's obvious knowledge, I agreed with him just on general principles. Whiffles did too, though he made it look like he was feeling a little badly about the idea of quitting. Still, the old rattletrap wouldn't run, so what else could we do? Surely the old man could see that.

But then we noticed that old Mr. Jensen was standing there staring down at us, his eyes all flinty and cold.

"Young fellers," he said slowly, speaking around the plug in his mouth. "If'n you don't learn nothin' else in your whole doggone lives, you'd better learn this one thing. A man hadn't ought to itch for something unless he's willing to scratch for it. If you ain't willing to push Lizzie a little, you sure as a certain hot place don't deserve to drive her. Ever!"

Then he spat on the ground in front of us, turned, and hobbled off.

Well, we sat and looked at each other for a bit . . . then Whiffles jumped up and, kicking at Tobe and shouting at the rest of us, began pushing on the Lizzie. After a few seconds we all joined in, and did we ever push! Up and down that field we went, back and forth across it, till there was no alfalfa left standing and we were all panting like lizards on a hot rock. And still that old car hadn't so much as wheezed.

Thoroughly exhausted, we all sank to the ground again, groaning and sweating and ready to walk away. It was downright wonderful.

"Well, young fellers," the old man squeaked as he hobbled up to us again. "That Lizzie is just like a woman. She's gotten more stubborn as she's gotten older. Has she got gas?"

"Yep," we answered in unison.

"Well, was I you then, I'd give her a bit more encouragement."

"Encouragement," we all groaned, once again in unison. If we hadn't been so darn beat that might have been funny. But right then we were too tired to see humor anywhere, especially in the old man. He was really starting to get on our nerves. I mean, he acted like he knew all there was to know about everything, and to my certain knowledge he hadn't made one useful suggestion since the day we'd first climbed onto his porch. He was a genuine one hundred percent wonder!

For a moment or so the four of us glared at him. Then we looked at each other, nodded, rose to our feet, and without even looking at him again we walked away. Just like we'd planned to do. For us, the Lizzie project was over.

"Quitting, huh," he shouted after us. "Well, I'll be go to a hot place if'n you ain't all quitters. It's too bad, too, 'cause I was about to tell you how to encourage Lizzie to go."

Well, we all looked at each other again, and then the Spinner noticed the look in my eye.

"Don't," he said, "Drop it!" But I would have none of his advice, not then. I'd enjoyed about all of that old man I could stand. Angrily I spun around and started back toward him, my brain in neutral, my mouth in gear and my tongue floorboarded.

"Encouragement!" I roared, ignoring my pleading friends. "Listen, old man. For three weeks we've done nothing but give that rusting pile of nuts and bolts all the encouragement we could. That and listen to you rattle on about doohickies and thingamajigs and other nonsense. Well, I'm tired of the whole deal! I'm tired of your spitting and your swearing and your car, and I'm especially tired of listening to your advice!"

"Tired!" the old man shouted back. "Why you chuckleheaded young colt, you got a head so hollow you'd ought to learn sign language so's you can keep away from the echo! While your buddies have been purty near drowning in their own sweat you've been standing around scratching your nose. I know, I've been watching. Most dumb folks I know was born that way. But not you! No sir, young feller, you've worked overtime developing your ignorance. Now you're right about my chewing. That's a filthy habit I wish I didn't have. Same thing with my words. But sonny, you'd ought to know that anyone whose milked cows or slopped hogs or worked with a tractor just naturally knows what the hot place is. That ain't swearing, it's just a fact of life! Besides, ain't none of them no worse than lying or cheating."

"All right," I shouted, kind of surprised by what he'd said, but still carried along by my anger. "If you're so all-fired smart, you tell us what encouragement to use on this old junk heap, we'll try it, and then we'll see who's so doggone dumb!"

By now we were all back to the car, and the old man hobbled over to the hood, leaned over, lifted a little door in front of the windshield, and stuck his hand down inside.

"Was I you fellers," he said, spitting at my feet and twisting with his hand, "first encouragement I'd use would be a little gasoline. In her, instead of on her. Lizzie always seemed to do better when she had some in her."

Mr. Jensen spit again, and we just stood there staring at him. He knew! Somehow the old geezer had gotten onto us. Somehow he had . . .

"I told you young fellers that me and Lizzie was friends. I know her as well as I do myself, purty near. You want to know how I caught on? Shouldn't tell you, I reckon, but I will. Gas in her tank sloshes — that's how you tell when she's near empty. You got gas there in the can, you said you'd put some in her, but when you were pushin' I noticed there weren't no sloshin'. So I tested you and asked again, and when you said 'yes' I figured you were all crookeder than a snake in a cactus patch. The looks on your faces tell me I was right. Why, I'm of a mind to . . . to . . ."

The old man gasped suddenly, grabbed his side, and then he slowly sank to the ground. For a moment none of us moved, and then like we were going in slow motion, we got Mr. Jensen into the car, gas into it, and the motor running. It seemed like it took us forever to get to the doc's office, but we finally did, and, muttering something about Mr. Jensen being a stubborn old fool, the doc took over.

Alone in the hallway we stood with our hands in our pockets, none of us daring to look the others in the eye. I had never felt so low-down cheap in my whole life, and judging by the looks on their faces, I was pretty certain my buddies felt the same.

"What if he dies?" Tobe asked of no one in particular. "Then it will be our fault."

None of us answered, or I suppose even needed to. Our thoughts were echoing loud enough for all of us to hear each other clearly.

"Blasted car," I thought viciously. "I hope I never see it again! I'm glad the old man caught us. I could never enjoy that car now, not with . . ."

"Boys," the doc called, "Mr. Jensen's asking for you. But please, no more than a minute. He's in a bad way."

For an instant we looked at each other, knowing what we were going to hear, and then guiltily we filed into the room.

"Mr. Jensen," I said, "I . . . we . . ."

"Be quiet, boy," he whispered! "I've got to talk fast! You young fellers tried to put one over on me, but I ain't as crazy as you figured, am I! Humph! And I was trying to be your friend . . . wanted all of you to be mine, too. Thing is, I caught on . . . too late . . . had the title changed to your names last week, like I knowed you wanted me to. Want you to know, though, that I . . . understand . . . Was young once my own self . . . You done a good job mechanicing . . . like my own son would . . . have . . . Sure do . . . hope . . . you . . . enjoy . . . my Lizz . . ."

ACCEPTANCE

As the boy walked back to his kayak, the churning clouds above him tore open and it began to pour, great slashing sheets of water which fled before the wind, obscuring even the closest cliffs. The boy had been exploring some interesting rock formations in the Grand Canyon and had told his friends to go ahead and set up camp before the rain hit. Now, as the rain whipped against his face, he felt uneasy about his decision. Perhaps he should have gone with them. Usually, he knew, it was not a good idea to be alone in a kayak, especially on the Colorado River. But camp was only a mile further downstream, there were no major rapids, and so he had felt safe. In fact, in that mile the only thing that could come close to being called a rapid was a little white water at Crystal Creek. He had laughed as his friends were leaving, even when Shadow had said, "If you're not at camp by dark we'll drag the bottom and fire a cannon."

By the time the boy reached his kayak, the Colorado was red with mud. It almost looked solid enough for him to walk on, except that it was rolling and would not make good footing. He worried, as he readied his boat, about flash flooding, but there was no indication of it, no indication at all.

Quickly he slipped into his boat and threw on his life jacket, more for warmth than for anything else. He adjusted his grip on the paddle, shoved away from shore, and effortlessly paddled toward the current. Though all seemed normal, he felt an uneasiness, an urgent need to get back to camp and to the warmth of the fire.

With a few brisk strokes his kayak slid silently and quickly through the red water toward the middle of the river. Once in the mainstream he sat back and relaxed, paddling occasionally to stabilize his direction, letting the river do most of the work.

The walls of the canyon rose steeply and then narrowed, revealing sheer ebony cliffs interlaced with veins of pink granite. As the boy looked down the canyon, one of the most beautiful sights he had ever seen appeared before him. Water, cascading over the cliffs, had created hundreds of magnificent waterfalls. Totally captivated, he stared in awe, wishing as he did so that he had not left his camera at camp.

Suddenly the boy was aware of the sound of throbbing turbulence, and he knew he had reached Crystal. Quickly he paddled for the tongue of the rapid, wanting to catch the current. Yet he worried, for there was an awful lot of noise for such a small rapid. "Echoes," he decided. "It must be echoes from the rain getting magnified by the walls." He'd heard of that happening . . .

His kayak nosed into the tongue and he caught sight of the rapid, and for an instant he thought his heart had stopped. He caught his breath, and the bile of fear burned his throat. Crystal rapid loomed ahead like a giant, frothing, churning monster, and was easily the largest and most terrifying rapid he had ever seen.

"Oh, no," he exclaimed, "Crystal Canyon's flooded! What am I gonna do? How can I . . .?"

He could see that mountains of water high as his father's haystack were pushing everything in their path downstream out of Crystal — stumps, trees, and granite boulders as big as cars. And all that water and debris had built up a huge pressure wave on the cliff at the opposite side of the creek, a pressure wave toward which he was flying.

I've got to get out of here, he thought as he struggled with his kayak. *I don't want to die. Not yet. I've got too much to do. I've got too many . . .*

He was too far into the tongue of the rapid to try for shore, and so his only chance was to slip down the middle, somehow avoid the pressure wave, and then hope he would make it. With energy born of desperation he turned his kayak toward the first wave and got set. Reaching the wave, he shot up the wall of water so quickly that his stomach turned. He reached the top and was tossed and turned, totally out of control, yet miraculously remaining upright.

Sliding down the front side of the wave and into the trough, he dropped into the next wave, where the water caught the nose of his boat and flipped it over. Desperately he tried to right himself, but the force of the water was too great. The strength of the wave was overpowering.

Dear God, he pleaded as he fought to control his tortured lungs, *please don't let me . . .*

And suddenly he was flipped upright, as if his prayer had been answered.

Quickly he gulped in a great lungful of air, and then he shot up another wave and the biggest hole he had ever seen opened up before him. He slammed to the bottom of the trough and was immediately buried by the force of the wave. Under all that churning water the boat flipped again.

Bracing and maneuvering with the paddle, he struggled with all his heart to flip upright. But it was impossible, and he remained upside down, swept along in the inky blackness of the angry river. His lungs were burning from the lack of oxygen, and although he struggled harder he could do nothing, nothing but slowly drown. Suddenly his head was spinning, and he began to feel curtains of darkness close around his mind. There was a rushing sound in his ears, and tiny points of light began exploding within his skull.

I'm dying, he thought frantically. *God, I thought you were in charge! I thought you . . . Dad said you could do anything, so save me.*

The boy was about to pass out when he felt a sharp crushing pain in his legs and stomach, and then he felt the kayak shatter around him. A rock had freed him from instant death, but had smashed his legs and stomach.

Air! He had to have air! Ignoring the pain, he pushed and stroked frantically with his arms, propelling himself, he hoped, upward, until finally his head popped above water. Spasmodically he gasped several times, and then more jolting searing pain shot through his body — another rock. Coughing and gagging, he did his best to grab more air, knowing that the river could pull him down again at any moment.

Heavenly Father, he gasped, *save me, please! I can't die! I don't want to . . .*

And then another wave crashed over him, sucking him deeper than he had yet gone, and then slamming his frame against solid rock where it held him pinned. Inch by inch he clawed his way upward against the boulder, struggling until finally his head was in the foam and spray of the surface and he was filling his lungs with wet air.

The boy knew instantly that he had been caught by the pressure wave, and the force of the current now held him pinned against the cliff face. With the tremendous force of the water crushing against him he knew that it would be impossible to push away from the wall.

His legs and stomach ached, and his head throbbed violently. Gingerly he tested his head with his hand, and when it came away bloody he was not surprised. And all the while the water continued to beat his body relentlessly.

Reaching above his head he felt along the wall of the cliff until he found a small crack. Jamming his fist into it he pulled himself out of the water far enough to relieve some of the pain in his chest. But still his legs tortured him, and now his chest was again hurting, but in different places and in different ways.

Breathing heavily, he hugged the side of the cliff, and he was wondering how long he could hold on when something bumped him in the back. Looking over his shoulder, he was astounded to see a shattered piece of the kayak bobbing in the foam behind him. Suddenly the pain and the helplessness of the situation made him burn with anger, and clawing at the water he managed to grab the wooden strip and shove it beneath the surface. But quickly the strip, like himself, was pinned against the slippery wall. This frustrated him more than ever, and so yanking the strip of wood up, he shoved it deeper. Instantly it was sucked from his grasp.

At once he realized what that meant. Somewhere below him a current had sucked the wood away, he hoped, from the cliff. If the current had freed his wood, then wouldn't it do the same for him?

Dear God, he pleaded, *I can't hold on here any longer, so I'm going under. You promised me in my patriarchal blessing that I'd go on a mission, so please don't forget your promise. You can't let me die now, you just can't.*

Grabbing a last deep breath of air he pushed himself under, fighting as he did so to keep from being crushed against the rock. The pressure was intense, and he strained to go deeper, to find that current. He was dizzy again, and his lungs cried for air. He knew he could not make it, yet still he struggled, struggled against the panic that consumed him. Would he be sucked away from the cliff? Had the wood been pulled away or was it still pinned against the wall farther down? Had he been wrong? Where was God? Why wasn't he being helped?

It was time to reverse his direction. There was no current that would suck him away, and he had to get back to the top before his lungs burst. His thoughts were hazy, and he knew he was about gone. Yet still he gave one more tremendous shove downward, against hope and reason, for there was no current down there to find. But then he felt a pulling sensation against his feet, and his heart leaped. He pushed deeper, and suddenly his entire body was seized and dragged down and away from the cliff. He was helpless now, and all he could do was fight his lungs and hope that the undercurrent would carry him quickly to the surface.

God, he cried out in his mind, *why did you let me get into this mess? I thought you loved your children. I thought you loved me! I can't stand this any longer. It hurts too badly, and I can't stand the pain!*

The boy's lungs were on fire, and the lights were exploding in his skull again. Fearfully, he struggled against the water, trying to reach the surface. But then, like a bullet, he was thrust to the top. Frantically he sucked air into his lungs, pumping them like giant bellows until the burning subsided.

He remained on the surface, but still he was being tossed, engulfed and battered by the waves as they carried him down the river. He had no idea how long he had been in the water, but to him it had seemed forever.

Finally, however, the walls of the canyon broadened and the waves melted and disappeared into gentle rolling swells. There were no more rocks, no more waves. He had made it!

God, he breathed, *I knew you wouldn't let me die. Now I've got to get to shore. Please . . .*

As he floated down the river, pain began to pour into his body, and he found himself unable to swim. The current was gentle but swift, and he was floating with not much more than his face above the surface. Breathing was difficult, for with every breath his chest screamed with pain. His only thought now was to see the campfire and his friends huddled around it.

Raising his head as high as he could, he strained to see the fire, to see his friends, but they were not in sight. However something was floating in the water just beyond his reach—the wooden strip. He struggled briefly and pulled it toward him, clutching it tightly in his hands. Then for a long time he just floated, not thinking about anything.

At length, the river swept him around a bend, and there on the shore flickered a campfire. His friends were huddled around it cooking, and as he drifted closer their voices carried across the water.

Raising his head again he tried to yell for help. But nothing came out, nothing but a low gurgling sound. Surprised, the boy sputtered and coughed up a mouthful of blood. Again he tried to scream, again and again, but he could make no sound. He could do nothing but gurgle and cough.

Dear God, he wailed inwardly, *don't let me die now. You've brought me this far, don't let me . . . I don't want to die!*

It was full dark now, the red eye of the fire winked at him from shore, and the boy panicked. Again he gurgled, again and then again, choking and gagging as he tried to yell. But it was no use. He was powerless to let his friends know he was there. He could see them clearly, sitting around the fire and trying to dry out. He was only a stone's throw away from them, but totally helpless, so close and yet so far away. Another moment, he knew, and he would be past them. Another moment and . . .

God, I've never prayed with more faith. I've tried to be good, and it just isn't fair. I can't die! You can't let me die!

Then Shadow rose to his feet, walked to the river's edge, and looked upstream. His wrinkled brow reflected his concern. Bending down, he placed something on the sand, and then he looked up the river again. The boy raised his arms as high as he could, hoping with all his heart that Shadow would see them. Intense pain shot down through his body, though, and his arms fell back in agony. Shadow stood motionless, still staring upstream, away from where the boy floated.

Tears filled his eyes and he began to weep. It wasn't fair, but he was going to die. He knew it. He could only stare at the fire and at his friends as he drifted past, knowing that they would never see him again.

Please, he pleaded silently, *Look at me! I'm here. Can't you see me?*

But they couldn't, and it was no use.

Heavenly Father, he moaned, *what is going on? Why aren't you saving me? What do I have to do?*

Then it hit him. The wooden strip. Raise the strip into the air. Desperately he struggled to do so, trying to scream at the same time. More blood came, and spitting it out he stared at Shadow.

Look at the strip, he yelled silently. *Look at the strip!*

As he watched, though, Shadow slowly turned toward the fire. The boy dropped the wood and sobbed, watching his friend walk away up the bank, walk away from him forever.

Dear God, he sobbed in total loneliness, *this is it. The river got me. I can't do any more, and you won't . . .*

For an instant the boy was silent, his thoughts experiencing a flash of new understanding.

You won't? Heavenly Father, does that mean that it is my time? That you want me to die? Have I been saying the wrong things? I guess I'm not afraid to die. It's just that I feel so lonely, so lonely and helpless. But if you want me to die, that's okay. You're God, not me. You decide, and I won't complain. You have the power, and I don't. I trust you, totally. I . . .

Shadow, at the fire, turned and walked back to the water's edge. The boy, watching, realized that Shadow had forgotten his cup.

Dear God, he said, *you decide, and that is fine. But if you don't mind, I want to try just once more. If you want me to live, then let Shadow see me.*

With all his strength then, the boy raised the wooden strip high into the evening air. Then he closed his eyes and, doing his best to smile, he waited.

PART THREE

PARABLES

As two fledgling fathers, we are in the process of working with our wives in the rearing of thirteen children, and, we hope, teaching them how to make appropriate decisions. Parenthood is an exciting but often poorly defined occupation, where the challenges are many and the solutions to most problems well hidden. In an effort to teach our children, we have found ourselves traveling frequently into the world of plants, animals and fantasy for teaching illustrations. The following parables, selected by our young ones, are, as Michelle and Joshua so carefully put it, the ones they liked "the bestest!"

WILLY, THE WILLING
WATER SNAKE

Do you remember last summer, or maybe it was the summer before, when you rode with your family past that quiet little pond all filled with moss and cattails? You know, the one where you saw the egret and the redwing blackbird? And do you remember how the setting looked so lovely and serene that somehow your soul sang because you had seen it? Well, one of the reasons why that spot had such beauty was that such a beautiful thing happened there. For you see, that was the exact spot where Willy the Willing Water Snake lived with his family.

Now, Willy was the eighteenth of twenty-nine baby water snakes born to his parents, and to be honest I never could look at all of them at once and say with any degree of certainty, "That one is Willy!" No, for I could just as easily have been pointing to Sam, or Fred, or Fritz, or even (and you girls must forgive me for this) Barbara, for that matter.

Still, every time I ever watched them for more than an hour I could always spot Willy. You see, he was a likeable little snake,

chock full of adventure and fun. And imagination? You have never
seen a snake with so much imagining going on! To Willy, every
clump of cattails was an enchanted forest, every lily pad was his
own speedboat, and behind every clump of grass reigned a
mystery, just waiting for him to find and dethrone. Literally there
was nothing that did not interest Willy, interest him in fact to the
point where all else was forgotten as he plunged into one adventure after another.

And I suppose that was also Willy's biggest problem. For you
see, where Willy saw enchanted forests, his mother and brothers
and sisters saw only cattails, and where he saw adventure they saw
only normal things (usually-to-be-ignored things) that filled their
everyday world. Willy always saw more than they did, and
because they either could not or would not see as he did, there was
conflict. Willy would see something and go to investigate, and
quickly the whole family would be upset and out of kilter because
Willy was out of line. (Snake families always travel in line, you
know — in line and in numerical order. That is the only way
families as big as theirs can keep track of themselves. It's like . . .
well, like your family kept track of each other the last time you
visited Disneyland. Remember?)

So it seemed like Willy was always in trouble, always lagging
behind, always exploring, always adventuring, always learning, and
always out of line. Now, I should tell you that Willy's mother
really tried to understand her son. She did her level best (and you
know how hard it is for a snake to be level) to see cattails as
enchanted forests. She made a great effort to see mysteries behind
clumps of grass, and she tried not to get upset when Willy wandered away from the family. Still, she did, and in truth it was not
really her fault that she got upset. For you see, the problem was
that Willy's mother loved her little snake-son. And she was concerned about him. She had lived long enough to learn that
enchanted forests could hide enemies, and in the midst of adventure there was often danger. Try as she may to explain this to
Willy, however, he just laughed.

"Mom," he would say, "you worry too much. I'm as smooth a snake as ever crawled. I can take care of myself as well as anyone . . . and maybe better. And Mom, if it bothers the other kids when I get out of line, just tell them to close ranks and leave me behind. I'll always catch up. You are the slowest slitherers I've ever seen. Mom, I may wander, but I always wander wisely."

"Perhaps so, Willy," she cautioned, aching with fear for her son who knew so much and yet so little. "But please remember to stay close to the water. Do not forget that in the hot sun you will dry out very quickly. That will leave you immobile, and so at the mercy of any other creature."

"Oh, Mom," he sneered, "how can the sun get any hotter than it is now, and do any more damage than it is now doing? I've been around for the longest time, and I've developed a sense of timing with the sun. It will never get any hotter than I can slither."

And so the day came when the sun busied itself behind a large cloud. Willy, slowly slithering with the rest of his family, suddenly saw adventure in an enchanted forest far from where he had ever wandered before.

Without hesitation he left the security of his family, who, as instructed, quietly closed ranks behind him and continued on their way.

"Oh, how great freedom is," Willy thought as he paused on the end of a swamp-soaked log. "Why should I be bound by the rules that have fettered my mother for so long? I'm a new generation, and as such I should be free to make my own rules, to live my own life. They say that succeeding generations improve with wisdom and understanding. How can we improve when we are bound by the outdated rules of our parents?"

And so Willy wandered farther and farther from the safety of the pond, secure in the coolness of the cloud and in his own ignorance.

Later . . . much later, when Willy was thinking of returning, the sun suddenly made an unexpected appearance from behind the giant cloud. Willy squirmed anxiously, trying to hurry, but he found that the harder he squirmed, the less he accomplished. He was indeed beginning to dry out.

Suddenly, above him in the air, he heard the terrible screechings of a red-tailed hawk. Fearfully, Willy looked up, knowing that red-tailed hawks love little water snakes more than any other entree on their dinner menus.

"Mother," he screamed as he thrashed frantically across the dusty, heat-shrouded ground. "Mother, help me!"

At that moment the hawk spied Willy and began its long flashing dive, straight for Willy's exposed and sunbaked back. Far away, near the edge of the pond, Willy's mother heard the terror-filled cries and saw the scorching dive of the hawk.

Instantly she ordered her family into the water and raced toward her son.

It was close, and many who watched felt certain she would never make it. At the last instant, however, when the hawk was just a few feet from the ground, the mother snake reached Willy. Without hesitation, she slapped him soundly with her tail, sending him tumbling end-over-teakettle down the slope and into the water. The hawk, unable to stop, slammed solidly into the sunbaked earth. Groggily it flapped to its feet, where it saw to its dismay Mother Water Snake gliding safely into the murky water below, where his dinner had also disappeared.

So the years have come and gone. From that day forward Willy was anxious not only to live, but also to teach others every law that his mother had given him. You see, Willy learned that despite the passing of time, laws and rules remain constant. Truths never change. From that time forth, Willy was the most obedient of all water snakes. He had learned that true creativity could best be developed within the framework of laws his mother had given, rather than outside of them.

And so now when you pass by that beautiful little pond, you will be aware that its beauty comes at least in part from the great lesson learned by Willy, who ever after was known as the Willing Water Snake.

PENNY, THE PUSILLANIMOUS PIANO

One memorable day a certain man, a creater of fine instruments, completed work on a concert grand piano.

"Ah," he said, stepping back and breathing a sigh of relief, "she is finished . . . and she is beautiful. In fact, never have I created such a masterpiece. She is worth more than all the world's gold. Thus, I shall call her Penny, a name symbolic of her priceless value."

Gently the old man placed his hand on her polished surface. "Penny, beautiful Penny," he said softly, "I love you like my own daughter, for I have given you my all. Off with you now to Carnegie Hall, for *there* your perfect tone will bring joy to millions."

Carnegie Hall, Penny thought, as the unconcerned workers hoisted her into the van. *I can hardly believe that I am actually going to the famous Carnegie . . . Ouch!*

In dismay, Penny carefully viewed the scratch that now extended halfway down her left front leg. For a moment she almost cried, but then she remembered that the scratch would in fact have absolutely no effect on her beautiful melodic tones. After all, she considered, *I'm still the same piano inside.*

The Carnegie Hall manager, however, felt differently. No sooner had Penny been unloaded than he began ranting and raving, screaming and hollering that he had been sent a defective piano.

Defective? Penny pondered. *Can it be true? Am I really defective?*

And though her scratch was repaired that very day, the manager never let her forget that she was a problem piano. As each pianist would come into the hall to practice or perform, he would exclaim, "Oh, what a magnificent instrument!"

"Yes," the manager would grumble, "but don't let looks deceive you. You can't tell a book by its cover. This is a problem piano."

Surprised, each performer would approach Penny skeptically, pick out a few bars, and then turn and say triumphantly to the manager: "Yes, I see what you mean. The tone is too sharp, or else it is too flat . . . or this note or that note is totally sour. What a shame, and in such a beautiful cabinet, too. Have it tuned, please, before my performance. It must be perfect for tonight."

Surprised, Penny would try even harder. "If I am too sharp," she would say, "then I must make the effort for flatness. On the other hand, if I am too flat, then sharpen up I must. I will be a perfect piano."

And so, in anticipation of each new performer, Penny would sound herself out and do her best to make the appropriate adjustments. The trouble was, Penny changed her tone so often that she quickly forgot what her true tone should be. The more she changed, the louder the manager yelled, and the louder he yelled, the more she changed. Penny had become a pusillanimous problematic piano.

At last, totally exasperated, the manager sold Penny to a small theater in the Midwest. Penny was being put out to pasture.

"So you can't hold a tune?" the new owner groaned as he drove away. "Well, I'm sure it can't be too serious, and our audiences are not very critical. Still, if it gets too bad, then over the hill you'll go."

Hearing these words only added to the guilt and anxiety that Penny was beginning to experience.

At the new theater she tried desperately to regain her tonal quality, but try as she might, she could not hold her tune. And if this was not enough, Penny found that her new environment presented even more problems. For you see, the temperature in the old theater fluctuated wildly. In the summer it was hot and humid in the day and cold and climatized through the night, while in the winter it was cold and damp in the day and toasty warm at night. In sum, Penny's environment had as profound an effect on her tonal ambiguity as did her drastically diminishing self-esteem. Penny, more pusillanimous and problematic than ever, caused untold grief to the managers of the old theater, for they could never keep her tuned.

At last it happened. Penny was sold at the Saturday night auction to a young Mr. Peterson and his family. It was a cold and dusty ride in the back of that truck, and Penny, totally discouraged and knowing she was worthless, several times considered casting herself out of the truck into the gravelly road below.

But then without warning, Penny found herself sliding to one side as the rickety old flatbed turned from the road and headed down the lane toward her new home. She had barely regained her footing when her strings keyed in on several voices shouting. *What? Can it really be? Yes, by jingles.* Penny sighed. *I think those are children down there. Children? I don't recall the last time I heard the voices of children.*

"Oh, mommy! It's *so* pretty! Can I play it first, mommy?"

"Yes, dear. Let me hold you up so you can be the very first one to play our brand new piano."

Hesitant little fingers depressed Penny's ivory keys. There was a pause, and then all of the children squealed in delight.

"Oh, mother," the oldest daughter sighed, "just listen to those beautiful notes."

"Yes, children, this piano is the finest of instruments. Why, it was built specifically for Carnegie Hall. We must treat it carefully so that it will always sound as beautiful and pure as it does tonight."

The days ran into weeks, the weeks became months, the months turned into years, and the family's enthusiasm for their piano never dampened. The home was always warmed with love and laughter, the humidity of contention was low, and daily Penny was polished and praised; for Penny, no longer considered a problematic pusillanimous piano, had regained her self-esteem. In so doing, her tone became permanently fixed. Yes, and in the years that followed, the beautiful instrument was fondly referred to by all who ventured down the lane as Peterson's perfectly performing piano.

SNAZZY, THE SILLY SNOWFLAKE

Early last winter, at the beginning of either the first or second snowstorm (I'm not certain of which because I was never told), a very unusual thing occurred. Way high, far up in the dark churning storm clouds, a rather different little snowflake was born. Now as to appearance she seemed quite normal; nor was she different from the rest of her fluffy companions in size. Yet she was indeed a different snowflake. For it was her attitude that was unusual.

Now all of you know about snowflakes, about how they always travel in close family groups. It is also common knowledge that snowflakes are more than unusually social and gregarious. They will, whenever possible, travel hand-in-hand and arm-in-arm, sometimes even in very large bodies, and once they settle into a home they crowd as close together as possible and hardly ever leave until they die (melt, that is). This is their nature, this is their law, and of course this is exactly what we all expect from them. That is why everyone noticed when this different little snowflake came along.

At first she was like all the others, tumbling down and having a good time, but then, when she was almost a teenager (that is, in the life of a snowflake she was almost a teenager), some snow crystals falling near her reflected a little light in just the right way and in just the right direction and this little snowflake saw, for the very first time, a reflection of herself.

Well, to put it mildly, she was amazed. Never in all her life had she imagined that anything could be so beautiful—no, that *she* could be so beautiful.

"Hey, everyone," she called, spinning slowly in front of her 'mirror.' "Look at me! Have you ever seen such beauty? Such form? Were there ever crystals formed more perfectly?"

"Why, that is right," someone said. "Look at her. She is indeed a snazzy snowflake."

"Snazzy," the little snowflake said. "I like that. I am Snazzy, so from now on I will change my name to Snazzy. Then when . . . hey, get back, you clumsy oaf! What is the idea, bumping me like that? Do you want to break off one of my precious corners? My goodness! Have you no respect for beauty, for perfect beauty. Back, I say! Get back, all of you! Beauty like mine must be seen from a distance. Back away all of you. Back away and behold."

And of course at such insistence all of the other snowflakes moved away from Snazzy, leaving her to twirl and swirl alone. Down through the clouds and snowflake years she fell, dancing and spinning alone, shunning the crowds who were joyfully associating with each other all around her.

Yes, she was beautiful, and yes, she was admired. All the more ordinary snowflakes said so, and whenever a crowd swirled past her there were many oohs and ahs as her beauty bedazzled them. Ofttimes one or more of the common people (who were really just as beautiful, you know) would twirl up to Snazzy and ask if she would like to dance with them. But no, Snazzy would not. How could people see her properly if she was swirling arm-in-arm with another, or group of others.

"No," she would shout, spinning away as rapidly as she could.

"Get back, get back and leave me alone."

"But aren't you lonely?" one would ask. "Don't you miss the company of other snowflakes?"

"Yes," another would say. "And don't you miss the fun we all have?"

"Or the things we learn together?"

"Or the things we teach each other?"

"Or the strength we give each other when troubles arise?"

"Or . . . "

"Stop!" Snazzy screamed. "Of course I miss those things a little, but not enough to change. Don't you see? I am better than the rest of you. I was born that way and must always remain that way. That is the sacrifice I must make so you may all see and appreciate my beauty."

"But you need us," several shouted in unison. "You need us at least as much as we need you. Don't you see that? Don't you see that you need our association in order to remain cold. Without us you will . . . "

"Silence!" Snazzy yelled. "You are moving in too close. Stop talking and get back. How can you appreciate my beauty when you are so close?"

Sadly then the other snowflakes withdrew, wanting to be her friend but unable to be so because she would not let them.

So over time and time again she continued to fall, always twirling and swirling so others could see her, always showing only the portion of herself she wanted others to see, always showing but never feeling the good and bad things snowflakes are born to feel.

And then at last she came to the ground, all alone in a large space surrounded by drifts and drifts of her peers, who were happy and excited and cuddly as they settled closely together into their homes. But Snazzy was alone, and suddenly her dance was over and there was no one around to watch or to keep her cold or even to help keep the ground cold so neither of them would melt.

So all alone in the empty world she had demanded for herself, Snazzy melted. Suddenly she was no longer beautiful, she was no longer crystalline, she was no longer a snowflake. She was being changed because she wouldn't change herself. She was suddenly a tiny bead of water who sat for an instant wondering what had happened before the thirsty soil drank her up.

LOUIE, THE LOOSE-LIP LION

Long ago, on the faraway plains of Africa, there lived a pride of lions. Now, from the distance onlookers might have thought they were seeing an ordinary, run-of-the-veldt pride of lions. But not so! This was a justifiably proud pride . . . schooled in the art of integrity. And therein was their greatness and their heritage. For you see, within this pride was found true kingliness and queenliness, traits actually rare among lion prides in spite of legends to the contrary. And that is why this story came to be told at all.

For you see, within this pride of lions there lived a young lion named Louie who simply could not see the value of telling the truth. Add to that Louie's ever-increasing tendency to purr out flagrant mockings of those in authority, and one can readily understand the concern Louie's parents felt for their dishonest offspring. To be blunt about it, Louie was becoming a very loose-lipped liar! Untruths gushed from his mouth like water from the spring. Why, it even appeared as though Louie gloried in deceiving those around him.

As an example of this behavior, or several examples if you will, Louie was constantly pilfering food from his mother's cupboard. This, of course, frustrated Louie's mother endlessly, for she never knew what food was on hand to drag out for the evening meal. That was bad, but nowhere near as bad as the fact that Louie lied about it. Glibly, he would tell his mother that he had not seen the leg of gazelle, let alone eaten it. And all the while he would be insolently picking his teeth with gazelle bone picks.

Another example of Louie's loose lip was that even though lions are by nature very confidential creatures — secretive, even — Louie was not. If someone shared a personal problem with him, within minutes he would be flagrantly roaring it about the pride. Needless to say, before very long no one was willing to share their problems with Louie. And that was how he became known as Louie, the lonely, loose-lip lion.

The weeks and the months passed with lonely Louie wandering and pondering, shunned by the pride, who, without exception, were tired of his dishonest ways. More than once Louie thought about becoming honest, but it was so much fun to deceive others and then to observe their reactions. Also it was very convenient to get something for nothing, and always Louie made sure that he stole from those who would miss it least. And thus in Louie's mind no harm was really done. But, oh . . . the loneliness of Louie's days!

Gradually Louie came to realize that his friends shunned him simply because they could not trust him. Trust, they said, was the basic ingredient of true friendship.

"What a misinformed pride," Louie would purr. "Friendship is based on fun, not trust." And to prove it, he set out in search of new friends — friends who could enjoy life as he had learned to.

Within a day, Louie's expectations were fulfilled. He had found not one, but two friends: Pinky the Prevaricating Panther and Bruno the Burglarious Baboon. And oh, what friends they were! All day long they chattered away, and all night long they were happy and . . . well, they were committing crimes of dishonesty against the citizens of the veldt.

For weeks the veldt was preoccupied with vandalism. No one was above suspicion, yet neither was anyone apprehended. And still the three nefarious companions enacted their premeditated schemes . . . working one area one night and another the next. Oh, what a plight!

But then Elmer the Exoteric Elephant, sheriff of the veldt, placed his big feet squarely in the middle of the issue, and with a nose for detail he began sniffing out the trail of the plundering trio.

First Elmer went to Louie's parents, who told him of Louie's escalating tendency toward lies and rebellion.

"Louie thinks only of himself," they purred sadly. "Like all liars, he seeks only personal gratification and pleasure, never thinking of the welfare of others."

Elmer agreed, and then strolled off in search of Louie's friends, or rather, those who had once been his friends.

"But no more," they declared with sadness. "We like Louie, but we cannot trust his tongue. With Louie, nothing we say is sacred, and nothing he says can be believed. He has become a loathsome and untruthful lion, roarily betraying his true friends in his search for bogus bliss. If only he could see that wickedness never was happiness, and that the wages of pleasure are eventually paid with sorrow and pain."

Sadly Elmer nodded in agreement, and then he left the clearing and began his quiet search for the querulous Louie.

Shortly after midnight just a few days later, Louie and his comrades in crime were caught red-pawed as they were brazenly stealing barbells from the jungle gym.

Louie was the first to be apprehended, and as he realized that it was curtains for his destructive capers he began loudly declaring his innocence. Proclaiming with a pointed claw that Pinky and Bruno were the masterminds of this scheme, Louie roared his plight.

"Sheriff," he said with innocent conviction born of literally months of practice, "these are your culprits. They forced me— said I would die if I didn't—to accompany them as they committed their nocturnal atrocities. Thank goodness you saved me! Get me away from them before . . ."

"He's lying," Pinky shouted, looking in amazement at Louie. "He's betrayed his friends!"

"I'll say he has," echoed Bruno. "He's a dirty long-tailed liar!"

"Oh, sheriff," Louie purred in mock surprise. "You know my family. You know I wouldn't . . ."

"Be still," sighed Elmer, as he sniffed disgustedly through his tired trunk. And then, shifting his massive form to include all three in his conversation, he continued: "Louie, I stopped believing you long ago when I learned that you loved to lie. I see no reason to listen to you now."

"And you, boys," the sheriff said, looking at Pinky and Bruno, "you shouldn't be too surprised by Louie's betrayal. I learned a long time ago that, among many other things, a sinner is *always* selfish."

OLIE, THE AWESOME OCTOPUS

With a tentative twist of his tentacles, Olie darted deeper into the murky waters of the black lagoon. Even for Olie, the most venturesome of his devilfish family, this was a treacherous area into which he was swimming.

"Oh, if only Olivia could see me now," he bubbled. "Awesome Olie, she calls me. Ha! Why, with a little effort I could really show . . ."

Suddenly Olie caught his breath in fright. Floating motionless, he somehow felt shivers moving up and down his jellylike frame. Although his eyes could see nothing, still the foreboding darkness about him brought with it an invisible danger so real that to Olie death seemed imminent.

He was just coiling for flight when the water suddenly swirled, throwing his rubbery mass against a clifflike formation, and before he could respond, the giant shark reeled past, closing its jaws on the hapless tuna which, at this moment, became a tasty breakfast for the massive form.

It mattered little that Olie understood himself to be the largest of any teenage octopus in his cove, measuring almost twenty-eight feet from tentacle tip to tip. Nor did it matter that he knew himself capable of squirting a black fluid through his siphon that would camouflage his departure from the hungry shark. His only thought was of the day he had lost two of his tentacles to the jaws of a similar creature, and of the fact that only now, many long months later, had those tentacles finally grown back.

And so it was with great relief that Olie saw, as quickly as its entrance into the cove, the departure of the most feared of all seafaring creatures.

As Olie turned toward home, his thoughts once again turned toward the many months he had spent convalescing in the sick bay while his arms had grown back. Why, during those long months he could not even muster a single date . . . let alone a date with Olivia. But now, now that his arms were back again and he was in full form, he could get a date with any of the cute little squids down on squid row, including Olivia.

And Olie liked dates! Not just date dates, but jetting-onto-passion-flats-and-trying-to-make-out type dates. These were his specialty, and all fifty species of the octopus family stood in awe of his smooth way with the girls and the interworkings of his tentacled tips. All, that is, except Olie's mother and father. As they well knew, Olie was pure as the driven surf. You see, Olie lived the Word of Wisdom. Never in his entire seventeen years had Olie imbibed strong drink or held a seaweed stogie between his beaks. Each night when Olie would return home from his nefarious escapades with sleazy squids, his parents would interview him regarding his personal righteousness.

"Olie," his mother would gurgle, "where have you been? It's awfully late, you know."

"Aw, mom, get off my back. I've just been with the boys down at the Sand Bar."

"Olie, have you been drinking clam juice?"

"Are you kidding, mom? You know I wouldn't touch that stuff. I'm a good kid."

"Well . . ." his mother replied, "I hope you realize how serious that would be. Neither your father nor I have ever touched clam juice."

"Yeah, mom . . . I know. You want to smell my breath or something?"

"No, Olie Ander, I trust my little boy. Now run along to bed so you won't be too tired for church. Remember, the bishop expects you to participate."

Olie spent the next day in church, being dutifully *righteous*. That night, however, he was once again parked on passion flats, encircled ever so closely in the enticing arms of Olivia.

"Olie, darling," Olivia purred, "you're *so* awesome."

"Yeah, Babe," he crowed. "I know."

"But, Olie . . . Olie, I just don't feel right about being here . . . Olie, please stop. Please stop, if you love me."

"Aw, come on, Olivia. You know I love you more than I could ever say, and I really need you to show me you love me as well."

Breaking away, Olivia darted into a clump of kelp.

"Olie," she sobbed, "I do love you. That's what is wrong. Bishop Sting Ray says that if two people truly love each other, they would do anything to avoid causing each other pain . . . that two people can't be in love and in lust at the same time. And Olie . . . I feel so unworthy right now that I can hardly stand myself."

"Aw, hey, Babe. Relax. We're not doing anything *that* wrong. We don't need to feel guilty. We don't smoke or drink clam juice, and that's all my mom and dad ever talk about. What we're doing can't be too wrong or they would say something. All I ever hear is the Word of Wisdom."

"Well, maybe so, Olie, but I don't feel right inside. So I'm squirting home, and tomorrow I'm going to talk to Bishop Sting Ray."

"Come on, Olivia. Don't do *that!* I . . ."

"Goodnight, Olie."

The next day Olivia followed her feelings directly into Bishop Sting Ray's office where she at last was able to share her remorse and then experience the sweet sorrow that followed.

It was but a week later when Olivia's sense of relief was accompanied with sheer joy as she saw a solemn and reflective Olie silently glide past her into the same office. Giving him a smile of encouragement, Olivia went in to the foyer to wait.

An hour passed, and then two . . . when finally the door opened and Olie emerged, looking more thoughtful and sober than she had ever seen him.

"Hi," Olivia said shyly, "I waited for you."

"Thank you," he quietly replied. "Olivia, can I see you to your home?"

Silently they slid out the door, each eager to speak, and yet neither able to find the words. When at last they arrived at her home, Olie was the first to speak.

"Olivia, dear, can you ever forgive me? I just let my emotions wander unchecked. I'm sure my parents assumed my understanding to be more, in fact, than it has been."

"We're both at fault, Olie," she responded. "But now that's in the past. Goodnight, Olie. And Olie . . . thank you for being you."

Turning, Olie waved good-bye, and slowly made his way home.

"Mom and dad," Olie said when he arrived, "I've got to talk with you. Olivia and I have . . . well, *had* some problems, and I've just been to visit Bishop Sting Ray."

Olie then burst into tears, realizing even more fully the amount of impact his actions had upon others.

"Mom," Olie sobbed, "what have I done? What have I done to Olivia, what have I done to you and dad, and what have I done to myself? What am I now?"

"Olie," his dad sighed, wiping the tears from his own eyes. "Olie, what you are is our son, and in spite of this mistake, we still love you. It is obvious to me that we haven't taught you as we ought to have done. That was our mistake. Can you love us in spite of it? Perhaps this experience will help you understand that parents are not perfect; they're just parents."

"And Olie," his mother interrupted, taking her son's face in her tentacles, "isn't it good that we can each obtain forgiveness for what we have done."

For a moment Olie stared down at the coral floor, thinking, unwilling to look at his parents' tears. And then, with the beginnings of a smile working at his sorrow-streaked face, and with the beginnings of a resolution working at his pain-ridden heart, Olie put his arms, all eight of them, around his parents, and together they squirted into their new relationship with each other.

DANDY, THE DEVASTATING DANDELION

The darkness was at last beginning to disperse with the first rays of light appearing as if from nowhere through the trees on the grassy slope to the east. This day, like perhaps the twelve or thirteen before it, was to prove monumental—not simply because spring was surfacing, although that was certainly part of it all; but because on this beautiful April morning seven close-knit, wide-edge families were sending their firstborn off on a life of their own. For such was the way of the dandelion clan.

Although to some they appeared a seedy lot, still they had many things in their favor. Roots were very important to them, and becoming established, upstanding members of the community was the thing they prided themselves in most of all. In addition they exuded confidence, for they considered themselves a chosen people. They were the first to awaken each day, and consequently they taught their young the value of a full day's work, retiring only as darkness prohibited further activity. It was perhaps this energy more than anything else that accounted for the fact that they were the first of all the plant kingdom to flower in the spring, as well as the last to close up shop for the dormant days of winter.

Now before proceeding with the events of this day, perhaps a word could be spoken about destiny. There are many who cautiously choose each thought, each word, each step of their lives, feeling dutybound to never lose control, but rather to make every act an act of profound programmed destiny. Others, it seems, climb contentedly onto the passing clouds of life, and allow the winds of chance to take them where they may, giving no thought to direction or purpose.

And so it was with the sixteen seeds who, this very morning, received final instructions from their great-grandfather, McTavish Dandelion. Now, it was not a secret that old McTavish loved his posterity. Nor was it a secret that he had favorites among his wide-edge, wide-spreading clan. And that favoritism was shown most toward a young seed named Dandy.

It wasn't because Dandy looked any different than the other seeds, for he didn't. It was just that . . . well, Dandy's attitude was superior. He knew he was destined for greatness, and old McTavish knew that he knew it, too.

And so on this day, while the fifteen other seeds were released with merely a hug and a vote of confidence, Dandy was detained long enough to receive special instructions from the wise and all-knowing mind of McTavish. When he had finished, Dandy nodded with understanding, pressed his head against the soft flower that was his mother, and felt of her love. Her color had once been a bright yellow, but was now graying rapidly with age. And so whispering farewell, he lifted his tufts, and without further ado floated away on the early morning breeze.

For dandelion days he traveled, scanning the countryside for a possible resting place. He had seen his sister, Doris, just briefly as he floated past a parking lot on the east edge of a large city. *Too bad,* he thought, *as he saw her struggling to be freed of the oil slick she landed on in search of temporary nourishment. I wonder why she didn't listen to mother, who more than once cautioned us about the dangers of spending time in unattended parking lots.*

At one point he caught a glimpse of Donald and Duane, his older cousins, as they dallied dangerously close to the exciting drainage ditch that disappeared ever so quickly into the culvert.

Silly seeds, he thought, *spending time seeking only danger and excitement. Oh, how glad I am that I have direction, and good it is to have such complete control over my emotions as I do.*

With that, Dandy darted directly south, his eye focussing on several large and spacious buildings. *Yes,* he thought, *those must be the ones great-grandfather mentioned.*

With an accelerated twist of his tufts, Dandy soared to even greater heights as he surveyed his approaching new environment. Never had he seen such beautiful buildings. Floating forward, he studied each one as though he had sometime, somewhere, seen it before. Onward he flew, becoming more excited and apprehensive by the second. As he topped a building he was startled to hear a strange buzzing sound, and then almost as if by magic people appeared from everywhere.

Thank goodness for all of those sidewalks, he sighed, looking down at the multitude of shoes shuffling from building to building.

Let's see, he questioned, realizing that soon a decision would have to be made. *Now, which building could it be? No . . . not that . . . ah . . . but wait . . . yes! Yes, that must be it, for great-grandfather said it would be the one with all the books stacked inside its windows.*

Without another word, then, Dandy arched his neck and peered nervously at the huge green lawn directly below.

Home, he thought, *home at last. Why, it is just as lush and beautiful as I expected. Now where should I . . ."*

With a start, Dandy glanced out of the corner of his eye, detecting an unusual commotion. There, directly in the center of the lawn, were two blades of grass waving with all of their might!

Could it be, Dandy questioned? *Yes, by jingles, I think it is. Why, those two blades of grass are beckoning to me.*

It took just a few seconds for Dandy to float effortlessly down, and how proud he was when he maneuvered so perfectly so as to land directly between the two excited blades of green, green grass.

"Er . . . hello, boys," he coughed, not knowing exactly how to begin a conversation with total strangers.

"Hi, Seed," the larger of the two responded, bubbling with enthusiasm. "My name is Glade, and this young sprout to the side of me is Wade. We're two of the friendliest blades on campus, and it's our pleasure to welcome you to the library lawn."

Immediately the two blades loosened the soil between them, and before noon Dandy had nestled himself securely into the moist and fertile soil between Wade and Glade Blade. Never had Dandy felt so happy, for never had he felt such a sense of belonging and purpose.

Time passed and Dandy quickly found himself growing, for he drank deeply from the fountain of knowledge that was the university. He also felt gratitude for the daily protection and nourishment Wade and Glade so selflessly provided. Time and time again they shrugged their blades in humility, explaining that grass blades were taught always to work together, caring about others.

As he grew, Dandy found that although his edges were ragged and not as neatly shaped as the blades around him, still he was totally accepted by them and not judged because of his differences.

And so Dandy advanced, degree by degree, quickly gathering strength and towering above the blades who had at one time provided such crucial assistance for him. And as they did, he was more than grateful for their support and encouragement. After all, they had made every opportunity available for him to achieve his full potential.

It was to the surprise of no one, then, when after days of endless effort Dandy proudly displayed his perfected fifty-six-petal dissertation—his first yellow flower. Proudly he defended his accomplishment, and what a contribution that flower made in the green community around him.

It was late in June, a warm and sunny morning, when the blades gathered in respect, and one Dandell Dandelion received his long-sought-after Ph.D.

As his seeds of never-ending influence spread to the far corners of the lawn, Dandy felt a sense of justified pride. Time and time again he would recall the words of his favorite mentor, who said, "There is no nobility in being superior to another person, but true nobility is being superior to one's past self." And to that Dandy would repeatedly ponder a phrase expressed at his commencement exercises:

> There is a destiny which makes us brothers;
> None lives to self alone.
> All that we send into the lives of others,
> Comes back into our own. (Edwin Markham)

With the passing of dandelion years, Dandy seemed to think less and less of the valuable lessons he had learned at the blade of his esteemed mentors. Instead, he found himself turning more and more inward, being caught up with his own importance. His mailbox as well as his signature now carried the title Dr. Dandell Dandelion, and whenever introducing himself, even to new neighbors, he would let them know immediately that he was Dr. Dandelion, and that he expected to be addressed and regarded as such. And so he was.

One early July morning, while snacking on some Morning Dew, Dandy dutifully began to pen some thoughts which seemed to be crystallizing in his mind. *It seems that I have spent half my life pursuing academic excellence. I feel a sense of profound destiny as I am a member of a select group with unusual perspective and insight. I must never mistake creativity for scholarship. Nor can I afford to become personally involved in the lives of my students, for therein will I lose much of the time I have allocated for research. Onward, good Doctor!*

And so the weeks passed, and as they did the lawn community felt more and more the effects of Dandy's arrogance. He seemed almost unaware that his ever-increasing dominance was choking to death the struggling young blades who had once crowded so eagerly to hear him speak. Occasionally he would hear whispers from others about the gardner, the master who ruled.

Foolish creatures, they are, he would think. *Have they no vision to see that I am the gardner here? I control the destiny of this lawn, and it is because of my insight and capabilities that this lawn is becoming so yellow and delightsome.*

And so, using the lawn as his forum, Dandy would conduct symposiums of superiority, crying to the impressionable young blades that they must develop a sense of intellectual balance, a sense of profound awareness which he himself had learned and now modeled so perfectly.

One day during such a symposium the true gardner appeared. He sprayed . . . and sprayed again.

It was over.

Dandy died in desolate dejection, truly a devastated, dried-up, degenerate and dethroned dandelion — ever learning, yet never able to come to a knowledge of the truth.

The moral is simply this:
> *Sowing seeds of superiority, degree by degree, has the*
> *potential of leading us down the slopes of uselessness,*
> *until at last we drown in the murky waters*
> *of the swamp of meism.*

PART FOUR

A DIFFERENT VIEW

As teachers in the Church Education System over the past several years, we have found ourselves deeply involved with the scriptures. Because of this involvement, we have gained an increased appreciation for the Lord, who through his scriptures directs us toward making appropriate decisions. Occasionally, as we are discussing one scriptural concept or another, we find ourselves thinking of possible ways which might be used by the Lord (or his representatives) to bring to pass that particular scripture's fulfillment, and thus reward, in one way or another, the decisions we have made regarding it. During such conversations we usually allow our imaginations full reign, enjoying thoroughly where they take us. Our concluding story is the result of one such conversation.

We hope that this story, as well as the ones preceding it, will enhance the success of your decision-making and will help bring all of us a little closer to our eternal goals.

A TOWN CALLED CHARITY

The Old Man

With a sigh of relief the old man dropped onto a lichen-covered boulder which protruded from below the shoulder of the road. For a few moments he sat in silence, his eyes tightly closed against the pain in his legs, and there he waited for his heartbeat and labored breathing to assume a more normal pace. Finally his old eyes opened, and he looked with a sense of wonder back down the hill which he had so recently climbed.

"Heavens," he said aloud. "Did I really climb that?"

The hill was indeed long and steep, longer and steeper than any he had climbed in some time. But the old man had had no choice, no choice at all—not if he was going to get to the other side. And that he had to do. It was his mission, and so he had climbed the hill. And the reality of this experience, like each of his others, helped him time after time to achieve success.

As he gazed down the steep slope a vagrant breeze plucked at his straggly gray hair and then wandered on down the hill below him, shifting the long grass in gentle waves before it. The perspiration on his forehead dried cooly, giving him a bit of a chill despite the heat, and from behind him in the grass a meadowlark trilled, once and then twice more. The old man, smiling at the lonesome yet happy sound, feeling thankful for the realness of it all, at last turned to gaze upon his destination, wondering and yet somehow knowing just what he would see.

There, down the road and just around the corner, nestled a comfortable town. As communities go, the old man could see that it wasn't very big, but then it wasn't what he'd have called small either. It was, well, it was just a normal average community. And that pretty well described the inhabitants, too. By and large the people—men, women and children—were normal average people. They were happy or sad, busy or not busy, good or bad, or whatever, depending upon their dispositions or else (and this was true more often than it ought to have been) what had happened to them that day. In short, the town and its citizens seemed to be about like all towns and all inhabitants of towns, and the old man realized that most folks would have felt pretty much at home had they visited there.

Grimly he tightened the rope that served as his belt, steeling his mind against the real hunger that gnawed at the walls of his abdomen. And he wondered, as he did so, if he would feel as welcome or as at home in that town as most other folks would have felt.

But yes, he quickly thought, he supposed he would. For there was one thing that, in spite of all the other common things, made this town very unusual. In fact, it was so unusual that the people, each and every one of them, prided themselves with it. And that unusual thing was, of course, the name of the community. For the town had proudly posted, along each of the roads leading into it, a large sign bearing the proud title Charity. Charity, the old man knew, was the loudly proclaimed name of the town.

"Yes," one woman would say to another, her voice filled with genuine pride, "we have named our community Charity because we love each other so much. If ever one of my neighbors needs help, why, I am there as quick as a wink to help them."

"That is correct," a man would continue. "In my store anyone in town can buy anything I have. And if they don't have the cash they can either charge it or write out a check. And," he would add boastfully, "I never *ever* ask for any forms of identification before I take their checks. In Charity we have charity!"

"That's right," two young girls would echo. "We go out of our way to be friends with the other girls in town, even the unpopular ones. We don't think we are any better than they are. Why, just because we are popular, that gives us no excuse to be uppity. No sir, it surely doesn't."

And so one could go from citizen to citizen, from old man to youthful boy to freckle-faced child, or from woman to daughter to granddaughter, and always the claim would be the same. "In Charity we care. In Charity no one wants and no one lacks and no one needs, for we all have charity towards all." And, day in and day out, they did. Men helped each other with their chores and jobs, women helped each other with their tasks and responsibilities, and children helped each other with their chores and assignments. No one failed school, because all helped the others; no families experienced difficulty, because all families helped and counseled the others; no jobs were insecure or poorly done, because all others helped and encouraged those who needed it. In short, Charity was a model community.

Or, at least, Charity was a model community until that day when the old man arrived.

It was well into the afternoon when he finally came down out of the hills and passed the large sign announcing that he was entering Charity, the most benevolent of all towns. The sun was high and very warm, birds were singing in the willows along the creek, somewhere out of sight a cow was lowing her displeasure or loneliness, the poplars and cottonwoods stood bathed in sunlight green, almost glowing against the deep blue of the sky, and the old man wondered at the miracle of his hunger and pain, hunger and pain experienced in the midst of so much natural beauty. But then he passed the first people, two women, and his thoughts of hunger became secondary to his wonderment at what they thought of him. As a man, these women decided immediately, he wasn't much and maybe he was even less than that. His clothes were ragged, his shoes were worn and full of holes, his hair and whiskers were long and scraggly, and he needed a bath. In fact he most definitely needed a bath worse than anything, as all those who happened to get downwind of him that day willingly attested. In plain words, as one good women hastily told another after he had passed, he *smelled.*

But the old man had grown used to how he smelled and accepted it as part of himself, for he didn't seem to notice, not at all. In fact, as far as anyone could tell, his powerful odor was the least of his worries. His greatest need, he seemed to feel, was located directly behind where his belt buckle should have been. In more plain words, he was *hungry,* and he wanted very badly to find something to eat.

So with more enthusiasm than finesse the old man astounded all who watched when he banged on the door of a particularly fine house, grinned a toothless grin at the particularly fine lady who answered, and asked if he might share supper with her family. The woman, aghast at the sight and overwhelmed by the smell, coughed and sputtered and finally slammed the door. The old man, startled, stood for a moment in thought and then went on to the next door.

On that door he knocked three times before the door was opened, and then it was opened by a boy. For a moment he stood staring at the strange old man. And then, in the midst of his request for food, the boy suddenly shouted.

"Hey, ma, there's a tramp here."

"A tramp? At the *front* door? Are you sure?"

"Yeah, I'm sure. Says he's hungry."

"Well, just a minute," the woman called, coming toward the door herself. "I don't understand why they can't go to the back door. Have they no resp---. Oh, hello, can I do something for you?"

The old man, watching her eyes intently, told her of his hunger and of his need. She listened, but as he spoke a tiny breeze came from behind him and drifted past the woman's nose, assaulting her olfactory senses. Her eyes widened, and at that moment the old man scratched an itch on his neck, a marvelously real one, too, and the woman was instantly convinced that vermin, vermin unwelcome in her home, were causing that itch.

"Hey, ma," the boy suddenly shouted, though he was standing directly behind his mother. "He sure stinks!"

"The woman blanched, embarrassed not by what her son had said, but that he had said it aloud.

"I'm awfully sorry," she said, smiling as sweetly as she could. "We were just leaving to meet my husband. Perhaps another time, if you should come this way again."

The door closed, and the old man thoughtfully directed his steps toward the front door of the next home. There things were going well for the old man until he got something caught in his nose. Of course, feeling an urgent need to breathe, he did his best, one way or another, to get the object out. True, his ultimately successful method was somewhat noisy, but still it surprised him when the man gagged and slammed the door in his face.

At the next door, besides the smell, he found himself stuttering almost uncontrollably, and that woman turned him away more out of frustration than anything else.

For the rest of the way through town it was the same thing over and over again. At one home he found himself so twisted up physically that he appeared almost inhuman, at another the lady at the door was certain he had a terrible disease, and always there was the terrible odor that seemed to surround him. So at every door in town he was turned away. The good people of Charity simply could not get past their eyes and noses and into their hearts.

The Boy

And so the old man came at last to the far edge of the town of Charity, still ragged, still dirty, still reeking, and *still hungry*. In fact, he was even more hungry than when he had entered the town, and that kind of hunger is not very conducive to happiness. Thoroughly

disgusted and disappointed he sat down on a ditchbank to con-
template, and there he was sitting when he heard a tiny voice
behind him.

"Mister," the voice said, "you look hungry. This ain't much, but
it's all I've got, and I'll share it with you if you want."

The old man turned and beheld a small boy, equally as dirty
and ragged as he, holding out a crust of bread.

"Do you live there?" the old man asked, nodding toward
Charity while he broke off a portion of the bread.

"Oh no! That is too fine a town for the likes of me. I couldn't
live there. I ain't got a home or nice clothes or nothing like that. I
live in the hollow over there, under the roots of that old cotton-
wood."

"Do these people know about you?"

"I reckon. They scold me often enough for coming into their
yards looking for food and such. Still, they're nice and don't hurt
me or nothing. And sometimes some even give me their leftovers
or their old clothes. Charity is a fine town, and a feller like me is
lucky to live beside it."

The old man looked carefully at the boy, determined that he
was telling the truth, and then turned slowly away.

"Son," he asked, "where are your parents?"

"Oh, long gone, I reckon. For a while they gave it their best
shot caring for me, but then it must have got too much for them,
so they left me here. They said a town called Charity sure ought to
treat a boy right. And it has, too. Think what it might have been
like if they had left me over by Perdition. I'll betcha that's a rough
place."

"Well, it is, in a way," the old man replied. "I was there once.
Town was named because it's so hot there, not because of the folks
in it. I did have a hard time leaving there though. A rough time.
Couldn't seem to get away from the people. They kept trying to
push food into me."

"Wow," the boy replied. "Who'd have ever thought that? Still,
Charity has been good to me. I've done fine here. I only feel bad
about one thing."

"What's that?"

"Oh, nothing, I guess. I just kinda wish I had some way of repaying all these good folks."

Again the old man looked carefully at the boy, and again he was astounded to see that the boy was being totally honest. He really wanted to repay the people for their goodness to him.

"Well," he said at length, "I suppose we could work that out. I surely do. It's a mite early, but that shouldn't matter. No sir, it shouldn't matter at all. Let's go, boy. We'll go into town together, you and I, and we'll give those folks a gift that would delight the heart of anyone."

The Little Town

Together the two of them strode into the center of town, to the town square, and right in the middle of the square the old man marked off a large space in the earth with a stick. With amazing rapidity he began working, and in no time at all passersby could see that he was making out of the dust, and water from the well, a mud replica of their town of Charity.

"Hey, ma," a boy would squeal, "that's our house. That one, right there!"

"Yes, it is," she would reply in amazement, as stunned as her neighbor that the tiny replica could resemble with so much exactness her own beautiful home.

"What are you doing?" the mayor asked, enthralled at the sight of his new courthouse being duplicated by the old man and the boy.

"Why, the boy and I are giving all you fine folks a gift," the man replied. "We're building a miniature model of Charity, so all of you will have a better view of your lives."

"Well, that is right neighborly," the mayor replied.

"Yes, it is," agreed the town treasurer. "But we hope you don't intend charging us for this, this work of art or whatever you call it. After all, you *are* using *our* mud and water."

"Charge," the old man laughed. "No sir! There is no charge at all. The boy and I will get ample payment when we see the joy in your faces."

Throughout that afternoon and on until dark the work continued, the old man working with untiring zeal and the boy helping as best he was able. At length all the townspeople went home to supper, but still the man toiled on. Later, as they retired, many looked out their windows to check, and sure enough, the old man was still working in the moonlight, building their town.

With dawn the first citizen out hurried to the square and stopped in amazement, unsure of what he was seeing. Hastily he aroused others, and shortly the entire town was crowding around, trying to see the work of art. For such it surely was. There was the town, built and painted exactly as it looked, with nothing left out and nothing out of place. The mayor's house, with its own flag-pole, stood just around the corner from the school. The model of the church actually had a tiny bell in its tower, just like the real one did. Hank Morgan's barn had a big hole in the roof, exactly like the hole in his real barn that the snow had caused the winter before, and which he had never taken time to repair. Why, even Agnes Terkleberry's screen door was hanging crookedly on her model home just as she knew her own door was hanging. In awe the citizens stared and examined, exclaiming over and over as new and tiny details were discovered and discussed. To say the least, that tiny town was the most amazing thing any of them had ever seen. The town, in all its detail, was perfect.

"But wait," someone suddenly shouted, "he made a mistake."

"No, he didn't," said another.

"Yes, he did. Look at these signs on the edge of town. He left the signs blank. He forgot to put Charity on them."

"Why, you are right. He surely did forget."

"But, so what?" asked a third. "The rest of the town is perfect. Why worry about such a little thing as that?"

"Why worry?" someone shouted. "Because the name of our town is Charity, and we want it recognized for what it is. That's why!"

"Well, that is a good point," the first agreed. "Maybe we can find the man and have him finish his task."

Quickly a search was made for the old man and the boy to ask them to finish and also to thank them for what they had done. But the two were gone, vanished, and not a trace of them remained. Well, not a trace except the miniature town which they had built, the town they had forgotten to name.

Declarations

It was about then that the mayor ordered that a fence be built around the model community to protect it, and then Andy Johnson suggested that a roof be built over it as well, to protect it from the elements. The mayor readily agreed that the roof was a good idea, saying so and praising Johnson for coming up with it. But then a very strange thing happened, something no one understood. For when the mayor had agreed vocally that the idea for the roof was a good one, he had thought something entirely different. And now somebody shouted, "Hey, there's a little sign on top of the mayor's house."

Well, it was plucked out, and to the delight of everyone but the mayor it was read aloud. "Stupid nincompoop," the sign read. "What's Johnson trying to do? Act like he's better or smarter than me, suggesting that roof? Wait'll next council meeting. Then I'll get him!" The thought was signed "The Mayor."

Naturally everyone laughed, everyone but the mayor, and he turned a deep red. For, believe it or not, that little sign said exactly what the mayor had thought but not vocalized.

"Who put that sign there?" he thundered, his anger and embarrassment quickly turning into indignation. "Have you no respect for the office of mayor? Do you not see that though I am not offended personally, I must officially take a stand in defense of the good name of my office? Besides, Andy Johnson and I are the best of friends. Just a few days ago he and I . . ."

"Say, would you look at that," someone shouted, rudely inter-

rupting the mayor. "There is another sign on the mayor's roof."
Quickly the man grabbed it and began reading aloud.

"Oafs and numbskulls," the sign read. "None of them have
sense enough to spit downwind. I can't imagine who managed to
know my thoughts, but it doesn't really matter. If I get angry
enough they'll all be properly impressed, and as usual they'll forget
the issue, trying to appease their mayor's genuine and righteous
wrath. And Johnson, that pain in the neck, had better watch his
step or I'll have his political head on a silver platter." Again it was
signed "The Mayor."

For a moment there was shocked silence, the mayor's face went
from livid red to ashen white, and finally, without another word,
he turned and stalked toward his home. The crowd, silent no more,
buzzed with wonder and mirth as they discussed how some brave
soul had dared to lay it to their pompous, high-and-mighty mayor.
Gradually, then, the show being over, the citizens of Charity began
drifting home to their chores and to their breakfasts.

A little later, when a neighbor's cow wandered into Mary Zinkman's tidy garden, she went out, picked up the animal's rope, led it
home, and politely and graciously explained to her neighbor that
the cow had somehow gotten into her garden but that no harm had
been done and she was happy to return it.

Imagine Mary Zinkman's surprise when that afternoon the
neighbor who owned the cow suddenly burst through her door
with a tiny sign she had picked up, she said, on Mary's roof in the
replica town of Charity.

"You old witch," the sign read, calling the woman by name.
"Why can't you ever tie up your cow the way it ought to be done.
Because of you my garden is in ruin, especially the peas. And I
love peas. But just wait till harvest. Then I'll ask you for most of
yours, and you won't dare refuse, because you live in Charity!" It
was signed "Mary Zinkman."

Mary Zinkman was shocked nearly to tears, not with indignation but with embarrassment, for those surely had been her
thoughts, though of course she had been careful not to express
them.

Later that day the manager of the bank wished for a hole to crawl into when somebody handed his personal secretary a sign picked up on his rooftop in the little town detailing his thoughts as he had watched lustfully that same secretary walk past him to do some filing. She was humiliated, of course. But she fled the bank in tears when a few moments later someone brought in another sign. That sign, found on her roof, detailed her plans to use her fine figure to coerce the banker into a raise. No one would ever know, the sign indicated, and her husband would be too thrilled with the raise to ever wonder how she got it.

Meanwhile, over at the school the students were reading a sign taken from the top of their teacher's home, a sign expressing her intense displeasure at helping her amazingly retarded pupils, for the umpteenth time that week, solve an absolutely simple problem she had given them. "Good merciful heaven," the sign concluded, "even that stupid boy who lives out in the wash could solve this problem." That sign bore her own signature. Naturally the students were shocked and surprised.

There were other incidents too, many others, as through the day little signs appeared here and there throughout the town, expressing in detail the secret thoughts of the citizens of Charity. And needless to say, it was a most embarrassing situation for almost everyone.

Late that afternoon the mayor received his first petition for permission to destroy the little town. But when permission was hastily granted and the man arrived to do so, there, being read aloud by his next-door neighbor, was a sign explaining thoroughly why the man *really* wanted to destroy the town. Of course he immediately backed off, as did all the others who had similar desires, but who were also exposed. And so the replica of Charity remained day after day and week after week, continually sprouting new signs to the frustration and embarrassment of the owners, and to the hilarity and enlightenment of their neighbors.

Of course there were cries of miracle and cries of hoax, and occasionally the arguments for each became very heated. But that occurred less and less, for the little signs that seemed to appear out of nowhere showed some thoughts that were quite interesting, quite interesting indeed. And when all was said and done, there was really no one who could explain how the little signs appeared or where they came from. It was simply a mystery which defied solution.

One day, much later and in the midst of a driving rain, a little boy coming home from school tripped and fell headlong into a deep puddle. Kathy Winslow, looking out her window, saw the accident, and heedless of the downpour, ran out and pulled the boy from the water. She took him in, dried and warmed him, and then carried him home to his anxious mother. When thanks was expressed, she modestly accepted them, expressed her willingness to help, and returned home. Imagine her surprise the next day to hear someone reading aloud the sign found on the roof of her own replica house.

"My goodness," the sign said, "you don't need to thank me for that! Anybody would have done it. You especially, Mattie. I know you'd have done the same thing for one of mine."

Well, when that sign was read there was no laughter and no smiling, but just a lot of wondering faces. The next time there was a need and one of the citizens fulfilled it, however, he examined the thoughts of his heart carefully before he expressed them to himself, and to his surprise he found that because he wanted to, he was actually thinking good things. And sure enough, those good thoughts appeared on a sign shortly thereafter.

Excited by his discovery, that man spread the word, and gradually his neighbors followed his lead and made the same discovery. It was not only possible, they found, but actually pleasurable to control their thoughts and move them into positive directions. Besides, it was obviously more pleasant having good thoughts read by their neighbors than it was evil ones.

Like fire, the attitude spread, and people found themselves viewing each other in totally new ways. The storekeeper, instead of thinking of old Joseph Hatch as a crook (which always appeared on his sign, no matter how hard he smiled at that same Joseph Hatch), suddenly realized that Joseph Hatch had never intentionally taken anything from him. He simply had a very bad memory, but was quick to respond when reminded. To the storekeeper's surprise, his good thoughts appeared on a sign, Joseph Hatch read it, grinned in an embarrassed manner, and came in to pay a bill he had obviously forgotten.

Even the banker, one day, looked at his secretary without any lust whatever, realized what a fine person she was, decided to give her a raise, and thought how lucky Tom Jordan was to be married to her.

Well, his secretary beamed when she saw the sign with those thoughts on it, and she not only tried harder to be a good employee, but she even became a better wife to Tom Jordan. He, of course, was thrilled to read her thoughts, made a few changes himself, and self-improvement became an ever-expanding circle. People were improving to please those who were improving to please them. The citizens of Charity, so long used to taking, desiring, and lusting after, now began to discover the joys of sincere giving. True, it was quite difficult at first, but the rewards made even the most strenuous efforts at giving worthwhile. And the people of Charity, one after another, discovered that the longer they persisted in giving, of themselves as well as of their means, the easier sincere giving became.

Ila, Nancy, and Rebecca learned that Gertrude was one of the most levelheaded yet fun persons they had ever known, and as a foursome their final years in school were absolutely delightful. In fact, Gertrude ended up marrying Hank Allpro, but that didn't bother Ila, not at all. For she had discovered a big good-natured fellow named Forrest Jones, and she suddenly found herself end-over-teakettle in love with him.

Sam Pinckle and Tom Nutfall, brilliant young men, learned of Limpy John Homespun's incredible abilities with financial matters. Because they already knew of his unswerving integrity, Limpy John became the third equal partner in a very prosperous business, and the three became fast friends.

In addition, criminals began changing their ways, neighbors began loving their neighbors, and religious leaders were able to set programs in perspective as they became deeply aware of the needs, desires, and skills of the members of their flocks. In fact, one day one such religious leader made local history when he defended a difficult and apparently erroneous decision made by a young man who was under his jurisdiction. When his sign was brought in and read to the congregation, it said simply: "I have learned that feelings are more important than rules, and people are more important than policies. I have interviewed this man thoroughly, have found his heart and motives pure, and I therefore support his decision. In my opinion, so does God."

For a time then the little signs seemed to come in spurts, a flurry of good thoughts followed by sporadic negative ones, followed always by another flurry of positive thoughts brought about by renewed resolutions. No one found the process easy, yet almost all found it exciting. It was an interesting pattern, seemingly random, but, as the weeks and months passed, the patient observer might have noticed a gradual increase of positive over negative thoughts, recorded always on the little signs in the nameless miniature community.

The Old Man and the Boy

And then one day, much later, long after memory had faded, an old man came to town. As a man he wasn't much, and maybe he was even less than that. His clothes were ragged, his shoes were worn and full of holes, his hair and whiskers were long and scraggly, and he was in much need of a bath. In fact, he most definitely needed a bath worse than anything, as all those who happened to get downwind of him willingly attested. In plain words, as one good woman hastily told another after he had passed, he *smelled*.

But the old man must have been used to how he smelled, for he didn't seem to notice, not at all. In fact, as far as he was concerned, his odor was the least of his worries. His greatest need, he felt, was located directly behind where his belt buckle should have been. In more plain words, he was *hungry*, and he wanted very badly to find something to eat.

So with more enthusiasm than finesse the old man banged on the door of a particularly fine house, grinned a toothless grin at the particularly fine lady who answered, and asked if he might share their supper with them. The woman, aghast at the sight and overwhelmed by the smell, coughed and sputtered, yet finally said: "Certainly you may. Won't you come in? And by the way, I'm sure you'll want to clean up a bit before we eat, so the bathroom is right down this hall. By the way, you look rather familiar. Is there . . .? No, of course not, but . . . Incidentally, is that boy out there with you?"

"Why, no, not exactly. But he does look hungry, doesn't he?"

"He certainly does. Little boy," she called, "would you like to join us for supper?"

The child grinned and entered the door, the woman beamed and showed him the direction to the bathroom, and as she turned away she wondered at something. No, she wondered at two things. She first wondered that the odor of the strangers had somehow seemed to diminish once they entered her door, and then she wondered at how excited she felt about the prospect of feeding two perfectly dirty strangers.

"Oh well," she thought as she walked into her kitchen, "this is nothing really. What is a little dirt? They are hungry, we have more than enough, and well . . . if one of my family was ever . . ."

And so the day passed as home after home responded in one way or another to the knock and the request of the grimy old man and the equally dirty little boy.

At one home the old man stuttered terribly, at another he scratched at vermin, and at a third he was twisted over into an almost inhuman shape, so grotesque as to be repulsive to most people. And always he smelled, or at least he smelled until he passed through the doorway of the home. His odor then seemed to vanish, though no one really noticed that until they thought about it afterwards.

Now, not always were the responses of the people favorable, but by far the majority of them were, and so the two filthy travelers (who never seemed to get a bit cleaner no matter how many bathrooms they were shown into, or a bit less hungry no matter how many meals they were given) spent well into the dark hours of the night being wined and dined and joyfully entertained by most of the citizens of the town called Charity.

Finally, however, they excused themselves from the last home, the last window grew dark, and the last sleepy resident of Charity smiled gratefully as he went to bed.

Shortly after dawn the first citizen to venture out stopped in amazement, unsure of what he was seeing. Hastily he aroused others, and soon the entire town was crowding around, trying to see the work of art they had come to appreciate so much. But no one could see it, no not one, for just as surely as it had been there, now just as surely was the little town gone. Nothing remained of the miniature community, nothing but a tiny sign standing right in the center of where the town square had been.

Hesitantly the mayor stepped forth, picked up the sign, and silently read it. Slowly a smile spread across his face, and then he quickly gathered the crowd close around him so they could hear what he would read.

And this is what they found written upon the sign.

. . . the rebellious shall be pierced with much sorrow; for their iniquities shall be spoken upon the housetops, and their secret acts shall be revealed. (D&C 1:3.)

Welcome to Charity!